Advance Praise for Mone_

"In his latest book, Peter gives readers needed guidance for surviving a complex financial future. His extensive career as an actuary gives him a unique perspective on how to reach long-term financial wellness in a 'wilderness' that holds different challenges and obstacles for every individual. This book empowers readers to plan for the predictable, and to be prepared for the unpredictable—without losing sight of the trail."

—Mike Kaplan, CEO, Rael & Letson

"In *Money Mountaineering*, Pete Neuwirth stands at the summit of a career devoted to real-world financial planning, and takes in the view. His observations on how to ensure financial wellness over a lifetime are based on his deep knowledge of money and probability, complexity and change, and the quirks of human nature. The book is funny, frank, and realistic about how to navigate financially in an uncertain world."

—Peter Cahall, Chief Executive Officer, CapAcuity

"In this erudite but approachable book, Neuwirth outlines six principles of holistic financial wellness to thrive in an increasingly complex world. Alignment with Neuwirth's six principles will enable each one of us to approach our futures to optimize the probability of achieving exactly what we want, knowing our capabilities, while realizing what we can never know."

—David J. Ballard, M.D., F.A.C.P.,
M.S.P.H., Ph.D., M.B.A.

"The path to longterm financial wellness, like a journey through the woods to a waterfall at destination's end, is a path best begun early. In that way, one can reap and accrue the many benefits throughout the journey. With this book, Pete has crafted a powerful and inviting trail guide for those seeking longterm financial wellness. The book is filled with personal anecdotes and historical context, taking a conversational tone that invites the reader to take that first step. Equally importantly, the book shines with Pete's actuarial knowledge and experience and reflects Pete's ability to view things from perspectives that opens new possibilities. This book is both an invaluable resource and an enjoyable read. The Six Foundational Principles it contains illustrate Pete's wealth of knowledge for managing the unforeseeable in an ever-changing financial environment. *Money Mountaineering* and the guidance within will shape future curriculum and financial planning practices for decades to come, yet it is written for every person. As an educator, a parent, and an individual planning her own financial future, I recommend it highly."

—Stefi Baum, Dean, Faculty of Science, Professor, Physics & Astronomy, University of Manitoba

"Pete's true brilliance shines through in this book, which reads much like an adventure novel, where we can't wait to get to the next piece of wisdom packed in its pages. Pete generously guides us through the financial world in a way that makes it not only easy to understand, but also fun and engaging, as he teaches us through storytelling. *Money Mountaineering*'s six principles give us the foundation we need to achieve financial well-being. As such an important piece of our overall health, I highly recommend this book to set us on course to build and maintain financial health over the long term."

—Christine Tozzi, FSA, Electronic Arts

MONEY
MOUNTAINEERING

USING the PRINCIPLES of
HOLISTIC FINANCIAL WELLNESS
to THRIVE in a COMPLEX WORLD

PETER NEUWIRTH, FSA, FCA

Post Hill
PRESS

A POST HILL PRESS BOOK
ISBN: 978-1-64293-833-3
ISBN (eBook): 978-1-64293-834-0

Money Mountaineering:
Using the Principles of Holistic Financial Wellness to Thrive in a Complex World
© 2021 by Peter Neuwirth, FSA, FCA
All Rights Reserved

Cover art by Cody Corcoran

Post Hill Press
New York • Nashville
posthillpress.com

Published in Canada
1 2 3 4 5 6 7 8 9 10

Dedicated to my father Lee Neuwirth, Ph.D. and codebreaker.
Thank you for teaching me how to separate the noise from the signal.

Contents

About this Book

After forty years as an actuary, I've learned that people crave financial advice. Not only are people hungry for guidance on financial matters, but they are also confused and afraid of the consequences of the decisions they need to make.

They have good reason; despite what the experts tell you, it is not easy to sort through the complexity of today's financial world. Figuring out how that world might change in the future is an overwhelmingly difficult (even impossible) task. Add to that the cacophony of well-meaning (and not so well-meaning) experts offering advice, and it is no surprise that many people are discouraged.

So, is this another financial advice book? Not exactly. Rather, this is a book designed to help you understand what *kind* of advice you truly need. My goal is to help you better understand the world of money and your place in it.

I want you to determine:

- What you can decide for yourself (almost certainly more than you've been led to believe)
- Where you need help (probably in different areas than you think)
- What trustworthy sources are out there (fewer than you hope)

This book is not for those who are "too rich to care," nor will you get much value from this book if you have no financial resources at all and worry about simply getting by from one day to the next. Rather, this book is for the vast number of people in the middle, those who struggle with the trade-offs between saving for retirement or making a down payment on a house. It is for those who can't decide whether to pay off a student loan early or double down and borrow more to start a business. It is for those about to retire who need to figure out when to take social security, how much to withdraw from their 401(k) accounts, and whether to downsize their home or take out a reverse mortgage to supplement their retirement income. It is for anyone who has a complicated financial life in which it's not only challenging to find answers but also isn't clear what questions to ask.

You won't find any easy solutions to your financial problems in this book. If you work your way all the way through, however, you may find that you will learn to ask the right questions and, as a result, begin to make better choices. While many of the concepts here are not intuitive, I tried my best to make this book practical and understandable by anyone who remembers their 7th grade algebra; knows the basic rules and odds in games of chance (or mostly chance) like craps, roulette, and Monopoly; and is not afraid to consider new ways of looking at old problems.

Think of the world of money as a dangerous and unknown mountain wilderness full of unseen perils, inhabited by wily predators of all sorts. You have found yourself stranded and lost. In addition to surviving and figuring out where you are, you also want to make your situation as comfortable and stress-free as possible so that you have the time, energy, and resources to make the best of your life.

Consider this book a survival guide for a hostile and unfamiliar environment. *Money Mountaineering* is not a "how-to" book in the traditional sense, but it will give you a map of the territory, identify the most extreme dangers, and suggest tools and techniques to keep in your backpack as you navigate your way out of the woods to a safe spot where you can pitch your tent and build a fire. I can't tell you where to go with this book, or how heavy a load you want to carry. What I can give you is a better understanding of how steep and treacherous your chosen trails are. I can equip you with a pair of binoculars, a flashlight, and a compass to know where you're headed as you continue on your journey.

As an actuary who has lived happily in this wilderness for almost forty years, I can't tell you to enjoy the scenery as much as I do or to climb the peaks that surround you. If you do join me, though, I would love to tell you what I know about the terrain and share some of the tricks I've learned along the way.

Foreword

What Does It Mean to Be "Comfortable" with Uncertainty?
(For financial wellness or anything else)

By Annie Duke

Pretty much any decision you make is subject to uncertainty—the dual influences of luck and hidden information. You decide, and then the future happens. There will always be things we didn't know and things we can't control in between.

Somehow—probably including reasons related to things I didn't know and things I couldn't control—my winding career path has always focused on studying the influence of uncertainty on human decision-making. One might even say I have been obsessed with it.

As a graduate student, I tried to understand it.

As a poker player, I tried to improve my responses to it to become a better player.

As an author and advisor to companies and professionals about decision strategy, I tried to help others develop practical responses.

And, on returning to the academe, I tried to understand it better.

I've recognized for a long time the importance of becoming comfortable in the discomfort of uncertainty. Great decision-makers get comfortable with the fact that the future does not come with a guarantee.

Because of the influence of luck and hidden information, the future is a set of possibilities, each having some probability of unfolding.

No single future is bound to happen. Getting comfortable with the indeterminate nature of your plans is a necessary component of successfully navigating your goals.

When it comes to personal financial wellness, uncertainty is a multi-layered problem. First, we are tasked with developing a sound strategy, starting now and encompassing, potentially, several decades all while constrained by the limits of our information. Second, we are tasked with finding ways to execute that strategy. This might sound trivial but it is, in many ways, more important than identifying a good strategic financial plan.

It's hardly a surprise that limited knowledge related to financial decisions is the first big issue. What ends up being a blow to most people is the impact of their lack of knowledge about *themselves*. With all the investment information available, it's probably easier figuring out what Disney or Apple is going to be doing a year from now than figuring out how to translate your preferences, desires, needs, and fears into the foundation for a financial plan that covers the rest of your life.

How will your immediate financial needs change in the future? Will you have more money or less in the future (potentially way more or way less, especially during some unknown future periods)? How will what you regard as "safe" or "risky" change, either because the world changes or you do?

This is the stuff of this book, and Peter guides the reader in navigating these hazards, starting with his first Foundational Principle of Holistic Financial Wellness: "Every person's values, objectives, and financial situation is unique and multi-dimensional. Therefore, make every financial decision consistent with who you are, considering the totality of your own specific financial picture."

The second issue arising from uncertainty, figuring how to execute and stick with your plan, also takes most people by surprise. Frankly, the entire field of financial planning might do people a service by re-branding itself as "financial execution," but I suppose that would cause its own problems if professionals in that field became known as "financial executioners."

Execution ends up being a much bigger, more common, and costlier problem than flawed planning, whether from financial wellness goals or goals of the more short-term and mundane variety. Nearly a quarter of New Year's resolutions fail within a week. Only 8 percent of people reach the goals they set in New Year's resolutions.[1] Anyone who has ever tried to lose weight will tell you that their difficulty wasn't finding a good plan. It was sticking with it.

It's the same way, if not more challenging, with personal financial planning. After all, no one attending to their finances intends to blow through their money. No one plans to panic sell. No one wants to get in on a financial bubble right before it bursts.

Over time, there will always be reversals in the market. Sectors will boom and bust. A crazy, speculative idea at one time becomes mainstream at another. Conservative choices can become dangerous and risky. These things bob up and down as if they are permanently changing. Of course, those fluctuations turn out (with the benefit of hindsight) to be only temporary, more often than not. But we don't have the benefit of hindsight in the midst of the lows and highs. In the face of those ups and downs, it is hard to resist second-guessing your strategy.

That's why individual investors frequently underperform the market, even when investing in funds that mirror the market. The S&P 500 Index has returned 5.62 percent annually between 1999 and 2018, but, despite the omnipresence of S&P index funds, the average equity investor's return has been just 3.88 percent, lagging 30 percent behind.[2] In periods of market turbulence over the past several years, equity investors

---

[1] Ashley Moor, "This Is How Many People Actually Stick to their New Year's Resolutions," December 4, 2018, https://finance.yahoo.com/news/many-people-actually-stick-resolutions-214812821.html?guce_referrer=aHR0cHM6Ly-93d3cuZ29vZ2xlLmNvbS8&guce_referrer_sig=AQAAAMWpWYSLl0mJX-HI804dli4eJjuktn6T1ITCIx4l_U0J_E-cY1qXQYIlTb73WVwJtTfOqEGa2Z TRp1O2GuhaLKxejg06XR4YNsEusKhWrc8gSUd0792M7dAMdpyih8IbJya Jyo4fYWSxnZcR8oWTdyNIO8G2Z76sQTBmuPK8Pvnh_&guccounter=2.

[2] DALBAR, Inc., *2019 Quantitative Analysis of Investor Behavior* (for the period ending December 31, 2018).

have repeatedly attempted (and failed) to time the market. The more the financial markets test investors' resolve, the more trouble they have staying the course.

Peter addresses numerous ways to deal with this uncertainty as well. His strategies for both aspects of uncertainty involve informing yourself as a means to (somewhat) narrow uncertainty. For the most part, though, he presents ideas that take advantage of things you *do* know and things you *can* control, or at least influence. These include scouting of potentially dangerous situations, developing responses before your emotional centers have been engaged by a potential threat, finding and engaging allies (among professionals and people you trust), creating accountability for your behavior and responses, and getting positive reinforcement for refraining from counterproductive action.

All these things have specific applications, helping you maintain a careful balance between, on the one hand, flexibility and optionality, and on the other, pre-committing to keep yourself from succumbing to your moments of weakness.

It's wonderful that Peter Neuwirth, with his background and expertise in financial planning, has found value in some of my ideas and applied them to personal financial matters. It's a joy for me to see the ways others translate, apply, and build on my work using the specifics of their field and their expertise. That's especially the case with *Money Mountaineering*—separate from my respect for Peter and enjoyment in working with him—because personal financial planning is such an important subject with gigantic consequences for millions of people.

Introduction

Holistic Financial Wellness—
Six Foundational Principles

My eighty-seven-year-old father doesn't like debt. Not one little bit. Growing up, he often told me, "Neither a borrower nor a lender be," and that is the way he has lived his life. He tried to pay cash for everything and made sure that our family was never burdened with debt other than the house mortgage. Now, deep into retirement, he is doing just fine; he owns his house free and clear. His disciplined and committed savings behavior throughout his career as a theoretical mathematician provided him a guaranteed lifetime annuity from TIAA-CREFF,[1] which, along with social security and Medicare, gives him and my mother a modest but reasonably comfortable (and low-stress) lifestyle. They don't travel much, but they have everything they need and much of what they want. They even have a bit of savings set aside in case of emergencies. In short, his retirement plan was just right—for *him*.

For many years leading up to his retirement and after, my father would ask for my opinion on his financial decisions. As a pension actuary with access to all the theoretical knowledge there is about how one "should" plan for retirement, I gave him plenty of advice, almost none of which he took. But those conversations, along with hundreds of others I've had with colleagues, clients, and friends about their financial situations, were critical to the evolution of my ideas about how to manage one's financial life.

Eventually, I concluded that most of the advice and conventional wisdom around retirement planning and financial wellness, in general, is not only often *wrong*, but more importantly, is rarely *fully* applicable to a given individual's situation even when correct. We are each just too idiosyncratic in our circumstances, inclinations, and objectives for rules of thumb to work. Beyond that, almost all financial wellness principles are based on severe oversimplifications and overly compartmentalized views of critical financial decisions—whether they are as seemingly straightforward as "How much should I put aside in my 401(k)?" or fraught and complicated like "Do I have enough to retire next year?"

A few years ago,[2] I started blogging about Holistic Financial Wellness and how, without looking at the totality of our financial situations—that is, *all* of our assets and liabilities, including known future income and expenses, and hard-to-quantify assets like education, skills, and future earnings potential, along with our individual goals, plans, hopes, fears, and dreams—we will never make the right choices to attain the financial health we all seek. For a while, if you did a Google search on "Holistic Financial Wellness" or "Holistic Financial Health," my blog posts, as well as a few of the actuarial presentations I've given on the subject, were at the top of the list.

Now the field has become more crowded, and many others are using those terms. I'm sure that's a good thing, because it is important for more brains and voices to enter the debate, as the result will undoubtedly be better answers and insights. However, I also worry that my voice is now getting lost in the noise. So, as we get started, I want to talk about what I mean by Holistic Financial Wellness and how I believe individuals (with some help) should think about it.

Financial Wellness over a Lifetime

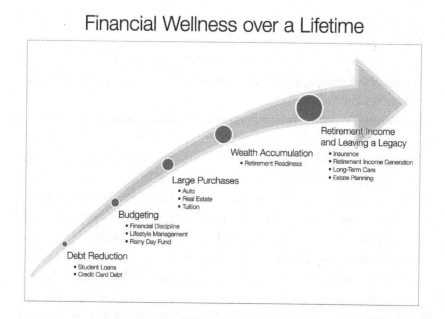

For me, Holistic Financial Wellness means ensuring financial wellness over a lifetime and doing so in a way that reflects your unique circumstances as well as your financial objectives, constraints, and values. When I say "values," I mean both what is most important to you *now* and what you are willing to sacrifice today to enjoy benefits in the future or protection against unforeseen circumstances that might arise. It is important to know how those trade-offs may differ depending on how *far* in the future you consider. In this book, our explorations of how to think about your money in that context will rely on six foundational principles. The first is:

Holistic Financial Wellness ("HFW") Foundational Principle #1: Every person's values, objectives, and financial situation is unique and multi-dimensional. Therefore, make every financial decision consistent with who you are, considering the totality of your own specific financial picture.

My Financial Path

Before we talk about the other foundational principles, I should tell you a little bit about myself, as I followed quite a different path than my father in the world of money.

Through most of my undergraduate years, I had no idea what I wanted to do when I entered the real world. With no particular career or other goals in mind, I devoted much of my time and energy to drunken house parties and Grateful Dead concerts, with an occasional study binge to prevent academic catastrophe. Because my father did not subsidize any of my extracurricular activities, I funded my lifestyle through multiple part-time jobs, each chosen to maximize income generation while minimizing time and effort. For example, I tutored some of my wealthy math-challenged classmates in calculus. I also became the resident super at my apartment building, which got me free rent in return for changing the lobby lightbulbs and shoveling the snow from the front walk after the occasional New England Nor'easter.

I went through college spending my time, money, and attention as efficiently as possible on the things that I enjoyed most. This was also true when it came to the classes I took, where I focused on quantitative subjects that I had a knack for, like math, economics, and accounting, while dabbling in areas that seemed interesting and not too difficult to master, like astronomy, linguistics, and anthropology.

Finally, in the Spring of 1979, due in large part to my father's generosity, I graduated from college completely free of debt. Leaving Cambridge, I drove my 1970 Toyota Corolla down to Hartford, where I started working as an actuarial student for Connecticut General Life Insurance. I rented a furnished apartment in West Hartford for $400 per month, and with my car running well, $450 in my checking account, and a starting salary of $14,000 per year, I felt like I was in solid financial shape. My father had also given me a stack of $50 US savings bonds that he had set aside bond by bond as I grew up to get me started. By then, the bonds were worth about $4,000. As soon as I got settled, I took them to my bank, where I placed them in the bank's safe deposit box given to me when I set up my checking account.

While I did not inherit my father's abhorrence of debt, I did pick up his budgeting discipline. Within a year, I had saved an additional $500 to go along with the savings bonds, building my asset base to $4,500. I also spent time learning the basics of actuarial science that year, including the theory of interest (e.g., annuities, bond mathematics, sinking funds), and listening attentively during morning coffee breaks as older students and actuaries talked about taxes, investments, and, most importantly, the financial magic of getting a mortgage and buying a house. With inflation (and therefore, house appreciation rates) running about 8 percent to 10 percent[3] a year, and taxes taking a disturbingly large bite out of every paycheck, the idea of buying a house looked to me like a fail-safe strategy to jump to the next level financially. The mathematics of the transaction seemed irrefutable.

To implement that strategy, I went house hunting and soon found a condo near the office selling for $45,000. My $4,500 was enough for a 10 percent down payment, and as my boss explained to me, my actuarial prospects were good enough that most banks would be willing to loan me the rest of the purchase price. I considered my future mortgage payments to be just a more expensive form of (tax-deductible) rent, so I viewed the condo as a redeployment of my $4,500 savings into a better yielding investment. The key for me was that buying the condo allowed me to leverage the impact of my savings; a 10 percent increase in the condo's value (from $45,000 to $49,500) would *double* the value of my investment (from $4,500 to $9,000).

The fact that at age twenty-three, I would be taking on $40,000 in debt—more than any sum my father had ever borrowed in his whole life—didn't even occur to me. For me, debt was not an emotional burden, nor did the risk of having that kind of liability on my balance sheet cause me anxiety. It was merely the right strategic move for me, with the upside dramatically outweighing the downside. The only aspect that gave me some pause was that I needed to come up with $6,000 in cash rather than the $4,500 I had in the bank to pay the closing costs and complete the purchase. But, having now been shown the magic of leverage, the solution to this problem seemed pretty obvious—take on more debt.

The *kind* of debt to take on also seemed obvious, since my girlfriend had graduated the year before with considerably more investable assets than my savings bonds. Although we had stopped dating seriously, as she had taken a job in another city, she was more than willing to lend me the extra $1,500 I needed, as long as I agreed to pay her back with 10 percent interest. This particular type of debt came with some hard-to-quantify psychological costs, but that is the nature of any debt we take on. It's another important aspect of thinking holistically about your situation. Borrowing from my girlfriend was the right decision for me. It made sense for both of us because I had a clear financial plan to pay her back while she could get higher than the market rate of return on a loan that she knew I would repay. Most importantly, the loan provided me with enough cash to complete the purchase and still meet the bank's underwriting standards for giving me the mortgage.

In retrospect, purchasing that condo in 1980 was the single best financial decision I have ever made in my life. As things worked out, I soon moved to Southern California, and in 1984, I sold my condo for $60,000. With the $20,000 in cash that I received, I bought a house for $180,000 in the town of Costa Mesa. Then I got lucky. The 1980s saw a boom in real estate, particularly in California. Over the next twenty years, I was able to keep trading up, one house for another, until eventually, the equity in the two houses I owned grew to nearly $2 million.

My actuarial career took me to several cities on the East Coast before I eventually moved back to California, where I live today. Through all those years, I've used debt to enhance my financial wellness—to leverage my real estate investments, as a buffer to ride through periodic cash crunches in my life, and to handle the (thankfully few) unexpected contingencies that have arisen. I have taken out many different mortgages and loans from my 401(k) and against the cash value of my life insurance policies, actions that would have been an anathema to my father and have sometimes violated the "rules" of many financial planners. Each time I borrowed money, however, I did so with full awareness of both the upside potential and the downside risk of the leverage that comes with debt.

This brings us to our second foundational principle:

HFW Foundational Principle #2: Debt is neither good nor bad but is always important—as important as your money or any other asset that you may own.

As we travel through the Money Mountain wilderness and learn what it takes to survive, we will start with a survey of the land and see why principles #1 and #2 are so important to keep in mind before you even put on your hiking boots or decide what to put in your backpack.

Understanding the World of Money and Debt

As complex and unique a financial situation as we each have, we need to make our way in a financial world that is almost infinitely more complex than our specific circumstances. What's worse, this larger environment is so complex that *no one* understands it. Even more daunting, its complexity can suddenly and unexpectedly turn against you in ways that are impossible to anticipate, potentially destroying your financial well-being or damaging your balance sheet in a way that might take years to repair.

And so, we begin the rest of this book by exploring the complexity of the world of money. We will talk about the history of money and debt. We will talk about how they each arose, the evolution that brought them to their current state, and how this world might change in the future. We will see how and why money was invented. We will describe the technological enhancements that have occurred over the centuries, including revolutionary ones like interest and debt (both of which were controversial when they were introduced) and more subtle ones like fractional reserve banking. The latter has been almost as significant as the former, but its full effects are only now being felt, four hundred years after it was introduced.[4]

Highlighting the importance of HFW Principle #2, we will specifically address debt and explore how it has expanded dramatically, both in extent and variety over the last century. Debt now comes in countless flavors (e.g., secured vs. unsecured, short term vs. long term, fixed vs. variable) and is just as complicated as and potentially more dangerous than the investment markets themselves. We will see that decisions with respect to what kind of debt you have and when/how to take on more debt have a significant impact on how prone to collapse (or dramatic improvement) your financial situation can become.

We will discuss how, in modern times, an accelerating array of innovations beginning with the idea of a public corporation with shares of its stock trading on an open market has led inevitably to a vast landscape of esoteric financial instruments and their derivatives. This, in turn, has created an incomprehensibly complex system of interrelated investment markets fostering entire fields of study and generations of PhDs in a variety of economic and finance-related disciplines, none of whom can fully understand, let alone predict, what the economy or markets will do—not in the next year and certainly not in the next ten years.

Most importantly, we will talk about how dangerous this complexity is to an individual. We will see that the financial world is like a rugged wilderness where ordinary people are left to make their way with little in the form of maps or experience to guide them. We will describe the terrain, identify the hidden hazards, and discuss where the unwary might get lost or expose themselves to predators that sometimes lie hidden in the bushes. It's a dangerous landscape, and as someone who has spent his career in the high country, I will share some of what I have learned in my forty years as an actuary to show you where the most acute risks reside and why all explorations of this wilderness need to begin with HFW Principle #1.

As an example, we will talk about how in 2008–2009, the almost incomprehensible complexity and fragility of the global financial system, along with the law of unintended consequences, inevitably led to a "financial forest fire" that nearly wrecked the world's economy. We will speculate on whether it could happen again, but most importantly, how you can keep your own financial house from burning to the ground in the next crisis. This is particularly important because your financial life may extend over many decades into the future; in that time, your situation, and maybe even your values, will inevitably change. Ensuring you survive a partial or complete system collapse and have the resources to change direction when and if your situation requires is critical to long-term financial wellness.

Armed with our first two principles of Holistic Financial Wellness, we will need to overcome the challenge of knowing who to turn to for help in making our way through this dangerous environment full of predators that are unfamiliar to most of us. Even those who make a living in the financial services industry are not experts in all the products, services, and transactions you may need to become involved with over time.

This brings us to our third foundational principle:

HFW Foundational Principle #3: It is important to take full ownership of your own financial situation. Know what you can't do yourself, and make sure those you hire are 100 percent on your side.

Where and When to Get Help

In the face of the complexity described above, our natural inclination is to seek an expert who can help us. Unfortunately, it is not so simple to find help you can rely on. Even determining the type of support you need can be problematic. As we continue on our trek through the financial wilderness, we will take a hard look at the purveyors of financial advice and the people you may have to work with to determine and implement your key financial decisions. Knowing who to trust and what to believe is *incredibly* difficult. Hidden, and not so hidden, agendas abound along with a frightening amount of incompetence. Costly mistakes can be made every step of the way.

The good news is that to survive and thrive financially, you don't have to understand the whole system; you only need to understand *your* financial world. As complex as it may be, it is orders of magnitude less complex than the financial system that you are a part of. Even to do that, however, you need to determine what you need to know about the key decisions you are facing while ignoring all the noise, lies, and distractions that can easily keep you from making good choices.

We will start our discussion by focusing on some of the most popular (and misguided) financial advisers that most of you have heard on TV, read in books, or viewed online. We will take a hard look at the real value of what they have to offer. We will show you their tricks of the trade and how many of them perform the "magic" that can so easily mesmerize you. After reading this section, my goal is that you will never be fooled by these charlatans again or be tempted to sign up for one of the "free workshops" that so many of these hucksters offer daily.

From there, we will talk about how to determine the type of help you need. In some ways, getting financial advice is like hiring a lawyer. Sometimes you need a lawyer for a specific transaction (e.g., buying a business). Other times, you need one to get you out of trouble or to find out if you are in trouble in the first place. No matter what, when hiring a lawyer, most of us want to find one who is an expert in the specific issue we are facing and then pay them a fee to make sure they are working for us and *only* us.

This principle applies equally to financial advice. We will talk about the variety of experts out there and how to find one who is honest, competent, and knowledgeable in the issue you are facing. In particular, we will point you toward some of the (unfortunately few) sources of information and analysis that *can* be trusted, and some insights and strategies that are worth taking the time to understand and apply to your situation. Because you may not just need information but actual assistance in analyzing and executing financial transactions, we will also talk about the type of advisor you should look for, how to find them, and how to use them to get what you need. Again, it is important to stay aware that it is *you* who will have to make the decisions, and it is *your* financial situation that must be fully understood and analyzed.

As I said at the outset, my goal is to give you a map of the territory to let you find your way instead of me leading you by the hand. I don't know how heavy your backpack is, how good your hiking shoes are, how high you want to climb, or how much risk you are willing to take to get to where you want to go. But once you understand your resources, constraints, and needs, you will be equipped to seek the help you need and make sure you can trust the advice you get.

Even with all the right equipment, you need to prepare for the unexpected. It's not enough to understand where you are and what is around you. You also need to know the changes that may occur (to you or the environment) in the future. Unfortunately, the future is *very hard* to predict. In fact, I believe that, fundamentally, it is *impossible* to know for sure what will occur as time moves forward. How to deal effectively with that uncertainty is what brings us to our fourth and fifth foundational principles:

HFW Foundational Principle #4: The future is hard to imagine and impossible to predict. Learn to live with uncertainty and have a financial strategy that has flexibility and optionality built into it.

HFW Foundational Principle #5: Organizing your financial life to survive a severe economic or life event is essential for long-term financial health. Strive to be antifragile.

How to Think about the Future

In addition to our financial system's growing complexity and opacity, the future itself is far more uncertain than most people realize. Despite the claims by some that Big Data will allow us to eliminate the future's basic unpredictability, mounting evidence shows that this is not the case.[5] Uncertainty and risk have been a part of the human condition for thousands of years, and all the technological inventions in the world will not change this inconvenient truth.

Uncertainty, as we now know, is woven into the fabric of the universe. In addition to physicists' discovery that we can never know if any particular material object actually exists or is where we observe it to be, it now seems that more and more of the complexity we see around us is the result of chaotic processes, those wonderfully simple algorithms that produce the beautiful fractal patterns that most of us are familiar with. The maddening and paradoxical aspect of chaos is that, even though there is nothing random about it, mathematicians have determined that it unfolds in a completely unpredictable way. In short, in addition to not knowing what chaos actually *is*, we will never figure out exactly what the future holds. Even our best statistical insights into what lies ahead will likely lead us astray.

As true as this is for the physical world, it is even more so when it comes to human events. Money and our financial system are *all* about human affairs. The concept of money and the financial system that surrounds it were invented by humans for humans. To believe that we can predict how that system will operate over time is a dangerous illusion that this book will attempt to dispel.

Happily, along with all the techniques that we have developed to manage financial risk, including a few that actually work, there has also been a great deal of progress made into figuring out the basic nature of uncertainty. This book will provide a survey of the geography of this mysterious landscape. We will trace the evolution of our knowledge of this realm, beginning in 1654, when the great French mathematicians Blaise Pascal and Pierre de Fermat decided to defy the Church, which believed that the future was God's domain. Together, Pascal and Fermat developed the basic principles of probability theory.

We will follow the evolution of our knowledge through the discovery of chaos in the last century and continue into the present, where traders like Nassim Taleb and others have expanded our understanding of fat-tailed distributions[6] that govern an uncomfortably large portion of our financial world. We will explore Taleb's concept of antifragility[7] as the key to surviving amidst this chaos. We will discuss how becoming antifragile allows you to actually thrive in a complex and potentially volatile system. We will explore this concept in detail and talk about how to structure your financial life, not just to be resilient in the face of stress, but to indeed get stronger through turbulence and disruption.

Despite our growing understanding of the nature of uncertainty, we still haven't changed our basic human nature, which craves to *know*. As uncomfortable as we are not knowing where we are, we are even more uncomfortable not knowing where we are going. And yet, we need to make many of our most important financial decisions with incomplete information about the present and almost no information about what the future holds.

To extend the mountaineering metaphor further, we will think of the future as setting out on a long backcountry trek where all we have is a map of the terrain and a pair of binoculars that will allow us to see a short way down the trail. Not only do we not know what hazards lie over the next ridge, but we also can't know what weather we will encounter as we proceed on our journey.

Fortunately, our current knowledge of the nature of uncertainty, and fat-tailed distributions in particular, can be used by individuals to manage the most severe financial risks and ensure relatively safe passage on the treacherous path that leads from the present to the future. We will provide specific examples of approaches of *how* to become antifragile, including adopting a barbell strategy that can provide a floor of protection against financial disaster while taking advantage of the dramatic upside associated with low-probability high-impact events.

As important as knowing what kind of tools to put in your backpack to prepare for uncertainty, what is even more important is to have the right mental attitude for living with the "not knowing." To help you, we will talk about the mindset of those who successfully live in the High Country where financial uncertainty rules and how those attitudes can be applied by the rest of us to manage our financial lives without falling prey to undue fear or complacency. In particular, we will review some of the techniques that poker champion Annie Duke describes in her wonderful book, *Thinking in Bets*,[8] about how to think clearly and make good decisions when you don't have enough information to be sure of the outcome.

As we think about our financial decision-making process, we will see that it is not just an aversion to living with uncertainty that impairs our ability to make good financial decisions. As human beings, we are all filled with emotional and cognitive "programming bugs" that prevent us from analyzing our financial situations and choices in a fully rational and dispassionate way. That is not necessarily a bad thing. Some of our irrational parts make life worth living and make each of us who we are. The important thing is to know what those parts are and be aware of the limitations and biases they impose on us as we face important choices that can have a large impact on our path to financial wellness. This brings us to our sixth and final foundational principle:

HFWFoundationalPrinciple#6:Financialhealthcomesfrom fearlessself-awarenessandacknowledgmentofourcognitiveandemotionallimitationsashumanbeings.Beclearon exactly what you want, what you are capable of, and what you can never know.

Knowing Yourself

As Annie Duke alludes to repeatedly in addressing the psychological aspects of making decisions under uncertainty, we need to recognize our limitations as human beings. Rather than think of ourselves as the "homo economicus" that most economic and financial theorists have historically assumed us to be, we need to embrace our irrationality. As behavioral economists have discovered in the last forty years,[9] we are driven by far more than economic self-interest, marginal utility, or even logic. When we make decisions, we are instead driven by fear, altruism, and a whole host of other emotions, some of which we don't yet understand. In my opinion, we should not try to overcome these factors. I agree with Annie; we need to become aware of them, but we need to go further and actually incorporate these very real drives and instincts into our goals and expectations when we make decisions.

To address this problem, we will first look at how wrong the conventional wisdom about financial markets and the economy, in general, has been. We will see how such outdated views persist and permeate much of what we read in the news. By reviewing what "experts" have historically said about the economy and how traditional economic theory has consistently been wrong when predicting where the economy and markets were headed, we will get a window on the anomalies that inspired the first behavioral economists to make groundbreaking discoveries about human nature. You will learn why it is vitally important to take expert advice on "current opportunities in the market" and "how you should invest right now" with a large grain of salt.

We will take a tour of the significant findings of the field of behavioral economics, including the seminal work of Daniel Kahneman, Amos Tversky, and Richard H. Thaler, among others. We will focus on the implications of their discoveries in financial decision-making and the financial world as a whole. We will look at these stunning insights into our nature from a somewhat different perspective than most current financial and economic literature. Rather than thinking of this hard wiring of our brains as flaws in our make-up, we will simply consider them features of who we are. The important thing is to understand our internal programming and how we might feel when the consequences of our financial decisions are manifested.

To address how we overcome our cognitive limitations and biases to make better financial decisions, we will again look to Annie Duke, who has developed many powerful techniques for "deprogramming" ourselves and learning to think more rationally about our choices. While she has described many of these methods in her books, here we *customize* those techniques, applying them directly to the important long-term financial decisions that most of us must make to achieve and maintain financial health.

Beyond recognizing that both the foundation of the economy and our internal processes are irrational, we also need to recognize that the *results* of the choices we make today will only be realized in the future. We will argue that while behavioral economics is now used to try and nudge us to behave in ways that "experts" believe we should, in truth, the only expert that matters when it comes to financial choices is *you*, because only you can really know how you will feel in the future—whether you will be happy, or the extent to which you will suffer from the consequences of your decisions. You will have to live in that future, so it is you who needs to take responsibility for the actions that will get you there. You will have a better understanding of the internal wiring that produces your thoughts and feelings, which should give you great hope for your ability to manage your financial life going forward.

Living in the Wilderness

If you've gotten this far, you might be hoping I will tell you how to apply these six principles to your own life. I'm afraid I'm going to disappoint you, because without knowing you as an individual, I wouldn't presume to tell you. In fact, HFW Foundational Principle #1 suggests that it would be the height of hypocrisy for me even to try. The closest I will come is toward the end of the book when I will share my thoughts about which tools to keep in your backpack that can be useful in that effort. For now, I want to "walk my talk." As Taleb says, *"Never ask anyone for their opinion, forecast, or recommendation. Just ask them what they have— or don't have—in their portfolio."*[10]

So, I will tell you what's in mine.

Even though my attitude toward debt is quite different, it turns out that I am very much like my father in my attitude toward downside risk and my tendency to care deeply about my future happiness. In a sense, that makes me a "low discounter;" I am very willing to absorb near-term costs in return for only modestly better future benefits. This has changed somewhat as I've gotten older (I'm sixty-four), but not as much as you might think. I also have a wife who is a little younger and much healthier than me, as well as a twenty-one-year-old son in college, so my planning horizon extends far beyond my own life.

In addition to my real estate purchases that I talked about earlier, I have been a consulting actuary for forty years, earning a good steady salary throughout. I was disciplined enough to put aside 15 percent to 20 percent of what I made every year. I was also fortunate to work for companies that were both profitable and paternalistic enough to provide me with a modest defined benefit pension. All of this allowed me to retire at age sixty and devote my time to areas of interest, only some of which provide any income.

So how do I deploy my assets and organize my financial life? The answer is by using lots of different institutions and investments. I diversify my risks by using four banks to hold cash and five different trustees, including large insurance companies and traditional investment houses, for our 401(k)/IRA accounts. I invest in a wide range of asset classes, including many underutilized investments like collectibles, alternative currencies, raw land, physical gold, and a panoply of financial instruments that are unleveraged but unlikely to all go down at the same time. I also use other more complex instruments that I understand and are designed to provide financial security and cash to my family and others through the end of my life and beyond. These include charitable gift annuities, a charitable remainder trust, and a large paid-up whole life insurance policy.

Regarding the ongoing management of my income, I employ a barbell strategy. I have three guaranteed fixed lifetime annuities (from different institutions) giving us enough to survive on for the rest of our lives even if we lose everything. At the same time, I also engage in three side businesses, each of which could end at any time, but have very high upside potential if I get lucky. We have one house that is our base of operation and a small farm fifty miles away where I spend most of my time. The farm generates enough rental income to pay its mortgage and maintenance costs and provide additional lifestyle flexibility if we need it.

Perhaps most importantly, I stay attentive, flexible, and willing to change my investments and income sources if/when our circumstances change. I also only use advisors for specific transactions and only pay for advice on a fee basis. When the time is right, and we have a better idea of where we might want to live out the rest of our lives, I will likely take out a reverse mortgage and eliminate much of our housing expenses.

I would never recommend what I do with my money to anyone else. It reflects my personal, idiosyncratic attitudes toward risk and the future. It may also be too complicated and require more ongoing attention than most people are willing to devote when managing their financial life. In short, I have customized my approach specifically for *me* and what *I* want, need, and value in life.

That's what holistic financial wellness is all about.

The Six Foundational Principles of Holistic Financial Wellness

HFW Foundational Principle #1: Every person's values, objectives, and financial situation is unique and multi-dimensional. Therefore, make every financial decision consistent with who you are, considering the totality of your own specific financial picture.

HFW Foundational Principle #2: Debt is neither good nor bad but is always important—as important as your money or any other asset that you may own.

HFW Foundational Principle #3: It is important to take full ownership of your own financial situation. Know what you can't do yourself, and make sure those you hire are 100 percent on your side.

HFW Foundational Principle #4: The future is hard to imagine and impossible to predict. Learn to live with uncertainty and have a financial strategy that has flexibility and optionality built into it.

HFW Foundational Principle #5: Organizing your financial life to survive a severe economic or life event is essential for long-term financial health. Strive to be antifragile.

HFW Foundational Principle #6: Financial health comes from fearless self-awareness and acknowledgment of our cognitive and emotional limitations as human beings. Be clear on exactly what you want, what you are capable of, and what you can never know.

SECTION I

Understanding
Money and Debt—It's a
Complicated World

Chapter 1
Complexity and Financial Forest Fires

The Financial Crisis of 2008–2009

It was September of 2008. I had just been transferred to my company's Paris office, located in a quiet neighborhood in the heart of the 16th Arrondissement a few blocks from the Trocadero. I had landed in France only a couple of months earlier and hadn't yet adapted to the French way of doing business, so when I arrived one morning at 8 AM (a habit I was finding hard to break), I found the office completely empty. With time to kill before my boss and the other early birds showed up, I made myself a cup of espresso. I sat down in my office with the European edition of the *Wall Street Journal*, the one English language publication that my company subscribed to.

The French are by no means lazy. Their workday doesn't end until well past 7 PM, and they also have a sophisticated approach to business, with more than a few large corporations maintaining their global headquarters in Paris. Yet, at that point, I still felt very much like an outsider. I was far removed from my everyday US corporate surroundings, barely knew the language, and had met only a handful of our European clients. I was also hungry for news from home. Even from across the ocean, I could sense that something important was happening in the US economy.

Throughout the summer, it had become clear that there were big problems in the US financial sector. Even though my focus was, for the first time, on a completely different society and economy, I picked up on the ominous rumblings, the increased volatility of heretofore stable markets, and the unsettling note of concern that seemed to be present in the statements of various government and other officials, most notably the representatives of the Federal Reserve and other large banks. Like almost everyone I worked with, I thought that the US residential real estate market was crazy and that there was a bubble in prices that would eventually burst. Still, I had no clue how much else depended on ordinary people continuing to make their mortgage payments. The eighty-five-year-old investment bank Bear Stearns had crashed and burned earlier in the year[11] (the pieces were picked up by Morgan Stanley, another investment bank), but like many of my colleagues, I didn't see that as overly significant, either. I had seen an equally old and well-respected firm, Arthur Andersen, go out of business a few years earlier (along with Enron and others) with no lasting damage to the economy. As far as I was concerned, the economy, and the market in general, was going through a choppy period, but I thought that nothing truly dramatic was likely to happen soon. However, that September morning, I saw an article about what was happening at American International Group (AIG) that shook me to my core.

At the time, AIG was the largest and one of the oldest insurance companies in the world. To an actuary, old-line insurance companies like Prudential Life Insurance, John Hancock, and Metropolitan Life Insurance Company are the bedrock of the financial services industry. Insurance companies represent the *ultimate* in sound financial management, even more than banks and investment firms like Goldman Sachs. Actuaries were at the helm in most of the big ones and had been for more than one hundred years.

While not as traditional or old as Hancock and Prudential, AIG was anything but a newcomer to the game. Founded in 1919[12] to provide commercial insurance to American companies operating overseas, the company grew quickly and, beginning in the 1980s, acquired several other medium-sized companies in different areas of insurance. By the

4

turn of the century, AIG was the largest insurance company in the world and was worth over $100 billion.[13]

By 2008, AIG had operations worldwide and provided almost every kind of insurance (e.g., life, disability, property, casualty) to millions of individual and corporate policyholders. If anything distinguished AIG from other large insurance companies, it was the extensive variety of products they provided. They were innovators, and whenever a new form of insurance was developed, chances were good that you could buy it from AIG. Like any other large insurance company, AIG had many actuaries overseeing the risks and liabilities that the company assumed each time they wrote a policy. And like any well-respected insurance company, I assumed that those actuaries were using all the tried-and-true techniques of our profession to make sure neither market volatility nor highly negative claims experiences threatened the company's solvency.

With that as background, I started reading about AIG's sudden problems with a relatively new and very small part of its business, the credit default insurance policies that it had been writing for several years. Credit default insurance essentially protects any bondholder against the possibility that the entity that issued the debt defaults on its obligation. I had followed developments in this area with some interest and even toyed with the idea of exploring whether such policies might be used by clients of my firm, who were worried about the security of pension payments from their employer's retirement plan. Such policies could theoretically protect employees against the possibility that their company would go bankrupt without enough money left in the Pension Trust to pay their benefits. It seemed like an interesting product. While it might be tricky to implement from an underwriting and reserving standpoint, I just assumed that AIG would never write such policies unless their actuaries had worked through the complexities and figured out a way to set both premiums and reserves appropriately. With a lot of curiosity, I began to read what the fuss was all about.

The article I read that morning described how, during the previous week, there were reports that AIG's credit rating might be downgraded because of concerns regarding its "financial product lines," specifically its credit default insurance policies. The paper then went on to say that

5

somehow over the weekend, the situation had gotten much worse. By Monday, it seemed that AIG needed an immediate cash infusion of *several billion dollars* to pay claims. To me, this was just plain weird and not the way the insurance business was supposed to work. Not only that, but within a matter of hours, the news got wilder. The numbers started to get bigger and the reports more credible. By midday, officials had announced that AIG needed $10 billion, and by late afternoon it seemed that the company needed $80 billion *immediately*, or they would go bankrupt the *next day*.

Investment bankers, along with officials from the US Treasury and Federal Reserve, descended on the company. They worked all night to craft a deal under which the US government agreed to give AIG $82 billion to get them through the day. The company eventually received another $100 billion, for a total bailout of $182 billion, far more than the company's actual value. In return, the government essentially took ownership of AIG.

How could this be? What sort of insurance product generated $80 billion in claims (over and above existing reserves) in one day? And how could such claims arise if no actual bonds were defaulting? Of course, there *were* millions of residential mortgages going into default, but at that point, I didn't make the connection. I wondered how such vast sums could move so quickly from one place to another without any further economic consequence. How real was this $80 billion anyway? It certainly didn't act or feel like any sum of money I was familiar with.

As I read more and more of the gory details, I began to get frightened. Something was going terribly wrong in the system, and it obviously wasn't just about an individual insurance company that had mispriced a new product or been a bit lax on setting their reserves. The foundation of our whole global monetary system seemed to be shaking badly, and one of the tall, seemingly solid towers of the system was crumbling. There was no doubt in my mind that this was just the beginning of something huge; the whole system of money had either become something wildly different from what I had always imagined it to be, or perhaps we were only now dramatically being shown just how abstract and ephemeral the concept of money actually is.

It turned out that my fears were (only somewhat) overblown and that the concept of money (at least for now) was still intact. In fact, AIG wasn't writing insurance at all, but was instead just making bets on the continuing real estate market rise. In a very real sense, they were engaged in a pure gambling venture, making gigantic bets that the US housing market wouldn't crash. They were operating their credit default insurance division like a race track bookie that tries to maximize earnings by accepting unlimited bets on any one horse without offsetting them with bets on other horses or financial resources to pay off if the long shot actually wins the race. In this case, the credit default insurance policies that AIG was issuing paid off at about thirty to one odds, and it looked like many of those long shots were about to be winners. How and why they were able to do that with no one finding out before it was too late is a complicated story about which whole books have been written (e.g., *Fatal Risk* by Roddy Boyd),[14] but for me, the more important question is: What was the fundamental cause for the crisis, and why did it ripple so catastrophically throughout the global economy?

In the ten years since the financial crisis of 2008–2009, there has been an enormous amount written about the fundamental causes and mechanisms that triggered (and accelerated) the collapse. Most of those accounts (e.g., *The Big Short*)[15] focused on the greed, ignorance, and "moral hazard" associated with a few key players in the system. The storyline that we are now all familiar with identifies the main culprits as the mortgage brokers and lending institutions that fueled the real estate bubble, the investment bank geniuses who turned ordinary mortgages into esoteric (and dangerous) financial instruments, the quasi-governmental organizations like Fannie Mae and Freddie Mac who "backstopped" the loans, and the rating agencies like Moody's and S&P who gave everyone their stamp of approval and obscured the risk level of those Credit Default Obligations (CDOs) until it was far too late.

As one might guess, in the aftermath of the crisis, many steps were taken to prevent a recurrence. We can debate at length whether those steps were the correct ones. In fact, I believe that they may very well be effective at preventing another real estate bubble-induced financial meltdown. However, as accurate as the postmortem on the 2008–2009 crisis might be, and as well-intentioned as the financial "reforms" have been, they could *not* prevent the next financial crisis from occurring. In fact, as we all saw in the Spring of 2020, the financial system came very close to collapsing once again. This time it wasn't a bursting real estate bubble that triggered the crisis, but rather the COVID-19 pandemic and the severe economic fallout from it that nearly caused the system to crash.

As compelling as the accepted narrative of the 2008–2009 crash is, I believe there is a deeper reason that a similar crisis was inevitable, and its moral is at the core of the challenge we all face when investing our money. There is a fundamental complexity and opacity that our financial system now embodies. There are several moving parts in the investment markets, and too many of them are interdependent in ways that very few people are aware of and even fewer completely understand. Even those who understand how the interactions work today will never be able to predict the evolution of the system and how those interactions might change in the future. Most importantly, *nobody* understands the system as a whole. It wasn't designed by anyone and it is not managed by anyone. And yet, it is a system we all must live in.

Nassim Taleb is, in my opinion, one of the world's foremost experts on complex systems and their potential for collapse. In his book *Antifragile*,[16] he describes three different categories of systems—fragile, resilient, and antifragile. Specifically, a system is fragile when it responds negatively to volatility in its environment (or the macro-system in which it is embedded) while a resilient system is one that is impervious to volatility, remaining stable regardless of the stressors given by the environment/macro-system. Antifragile systems, on the other hand, get *stronger* under volatility. One straightforward example of an antifragile system is that of the human body, which (within certain ranges), gets stronger and healthier when subjected to environmental stress. For example, a child's immune system gets stronger after exposure to certain diseases, and our muscles grow when we are forced to exercise. With this framework in place, Taleb explores and explains many phenomena that we observe, but consistently misunderstand. He describes how these misunderstandings can lead to spectacularly bad decisions.

I believe that Taleb's book should be read by anyone who is involved in managing risk. Later in the book we will revisit this concept of antifragility and what an individual can do to adopt HFW Principle #5 and organize their financial world in a way to be not just resilient but antifragile as well. For now, let's talk more about complexity.

How Fragile Are We and Can It Happen Again?

In 1986, after the Challenger Space Shuttle blew up, a massive analysis of what had happened ensued. At the direction of then President Reagan, a special task force (the Rogers Commission)[17] was formed, and NASA was directed to provide the resources necessary to determine the cause of the explosion. In spite of internal resistance and a skeptical press, they did a spectacular job, and in less than five months, the Commission succeeded in determining the precise reason for the disaster and how to make sure it didn't happen again. Many may remember watching the brilliant physicist Richard Feynman prove in a dramatic demonstration[18] before Congress that it was a frozen O-ring that had caused the problem. The Commission concluded that, if that possibility had been anticipated, and the launch had been postponed until the day got warmer (it was unseasonably cold in Florida on the day of the launch), the catastrophe would never have occurred. As a result of Professor Feynman's insight, many changes were made to the shuttle as well as to the launch procedures to ensure that no similar disaster would ever occur again.

And for seventeen years, the system worked—until it didn't.

In 2003, as the Columbia Space Shuttle lifted off, a random bit of foam flew off one of its external fuel tanks and struck the wing of the quickly-ascending spacecraft. Sixteen days later, as the shuttle was beginning its return to Earth, the ship broke into pieces and burned up well before landing, killing all aboard.[19] It was later determined that during reentry, a slow bleed of atmospheric gases coming though the tiny hole in the wing created by the foam's initial impact had caused the disaster.

In both shuttle disasters, clearly documented and avoidable design or process flaws caused the catastrophe. But the real problem was not a failure to anticipate, but rather the complex nature of the system that the space shuttle represents. All complex systems are, by their nature, prone to unanticipated combinations of circumstances (some extremely unlikely) that can conspire to bring the system down. Engineers have known this for decades and use many techniques to protect against these completely unpredictable (by humans) events.

From the Space Shuttle and public transportation systems to the power grid that keeps our lights on, our human-designed systems are extremely complicated. When any of those systems crash, disruption—or worse—ensues. They are, in Taleb's terminology, *fragile*.[20] By and large, however, despite this fragility, those systems work well. Even more importantly, when failures occur, they are usually not catastrophic. This is because safeguards, redundancies, and an enormous amount of contingency planning are built into the systems themselves. These techniques have reduced, but not eliminated, the system's fragility.

Beyond the reduced fragility, the design features above mean that when the system fails, recovery is relatively straightforward, and it is back to functioning relatively quickly. This is because the systems are well understood and don't change, or if they do change, they do so in a largely deterministic way. As we saw with the shuttle disasters, in many complicated human-designed systems, disasters do occur because of their fragility and the randomness associated with the impact of the external environment on the system (technically, randomness plus long periods of time equals volatility). This fragility can't be eliminated, but at least it can be measured, and steps can be taken to minimize it. Generally, however, such systems *can't* be made antifragile (i.e., we can't design them to be made stronger by random stresses).

There are other systems, however, like the human body or Earth itself, that are not a product of human design, but instead have come about through natural evolution. These systems cannot be completely understood by humans, and they change in dynamic and unpredictable ways. Taleb discusses in depth how those changes can occur and why we can never predict them, but for now, it is important to realize that evolved complex systems are *fundamentally different* from the systems we consciously design, create, and then manage. Being a qualitatively different sort of system means that while some of the techniques described above (e.g., redundancy, contingency planning, among others) can be useful, different approaches and attitudes are required to avoid (or survive) catastrophic failure.

The science behind what it takes to maintain, or more accurately not destroy (or be destroyed by), such systems is still relatively early in its development. It turns out that actuaries have considered this problem for several hundred years, but only from the perspective of how to keep a (fragile) business enterprise like an insurance company from succumbing to the stresses posed by a complex macro-system like our global financial system. Despite what some actuaries might suggest, almost all risk management techniques are pragmatic rather than theoretical in nature and were developed over many years of trial and error. That actuaries have historically been among the most successful professions in managing risk (systemic and otherwise) and have kept many large insurance companies solvent for over one hundred years is a point of some pride for me and others in the field.

Though Taleb hasn't called out actuaries specifically, he clearly has great respect for pragmatic risk management and for those who have long track records of doing it successfully (i.e., surviving). He has also looked at the problem of complexity from a deep theoretical perspective. One of his key insights is that when your system's survival or livelihood depends on a macro-system of this nature, your focus should not be on trying to understand the macro-system but rather on understanding your *relationship* to the macro-system in which you or your system is embedded. In particular, you should pay attention to how you respond to the stresses, unpredictability, and volatility inherent in such a macro-system. The point is that you don't have to worry about the macro-system itself; most large naturally-evolved systems (such as the Amazon rainforests) have reached a point, sans human intervention, of antifragility.

It really is the interaction of your system with the macro-system in which you operate that you have to worry about. This is why HFW Principles #1 and #2 are so important. Principle #1 exists because your system is *unique* and only you can know all of its details. Principle #2 is important because debt is what makes you fragile. As noted, we will talk about principle #5 and antifragility in much greater depth later after we have delved more deeply into the nature of uncertainty in general. That and a discussion of principles #3 and #4 will lay the foundation for building a strategy that can make your financial situation antifragile.

Now I want to turn our attention to the question of exactly what kind of system is our system of money. Is it like the Paris Metro or our power grid, a complicated transportation/transmission system designed by people? Is it naturally evolved and impossibly complex, like the Amazon rainforest? Is it fragile like the Space Shuttle, where the only hope for the short-term survival of its human passengers is redundancy and extreme vigilance, while at the same time accepting that eventually, there will be a total and complete failure destroying all the systems (human and otherwise) within it? Or is it antifragile like the human body, where a wide range of stresses only make the system stronger?

The answer is that our global financial system is an evolved and impossibly complex system, one that began with a human-designed technology (metal money). It has been tampered with over the centuries and enhanced by the introduction of more and more human inventions. In short, it's a hybrid. In many ways, it has the worst features of both types of systems; like a naturally evolving system, it is too complex, dynamic, and opaque for us to understand and predict. On the other hand, it is like a human-designed system that does not operate at a natural sustainable equilibrium. It has an uncomfortable degree of fragility and appears to need constant human management to keep its potential collapse from destroying all the important systems (e.g., companies and communities) embedded in it.

And so, we stumble along inventing new and better technologies (e.g., the Federal Reserve) that have, thus far, prevented the worst from occurring. Despite all of the brilliant minds who have devoted vast amounts of study and thought to the fields of economics and finance, the real question remains unanswered: How fragile is our global financial system, and could it collapse completely?

Certainly, the Fed managed to stave off disaster during the 2008–2009 crisis and has probably done it again during the 2020 pandemic. However, if they are unable to do so next time, we could face a truly catastrophic situation, including the complete demise of money and a reversion to the barter system that governed commercial life for several thousand years before money was invented.

In many ways, the world of money is similar to our physical modern world, where we have tampered with the naturally evolving Earth and upset its sustainable equilibrium. I live in a part of California where I don't believe nature ever intended so many humans to reside. In order to be there, we have cut down trees and built cities with sprawling suburbs, while allowing the wilderness surrounding those suburbs to grow unchecked. Then we dammed and drained the rivers to get the water we need to sustain ourselves. Every once in a while, lightning will strike a tree in the dry, overgrown woods around us, and fires race across the landscape, threatening to consume us and everything we've built. We have gotten very good at putting those forest fires out, and we now take steps to minimize and suppress future fires. Perhaps that is what we need to do to survive; our world is now a dangerous place to live, and the system is no longer in balance. In Taleb's terms, we have taken an antifragile system and, with our tinkering, have made it fragile and prone to collapse.

As I said at the outset, I have no answers for how to fix the global financial system as a whole, if it even needs fixing. However, I think that the financial crisis of 2008–2009 and the pandemic of 2020 bear an uncanny resemblance to a raging wildfire. In both instances, our monetary system was only saved thanks to extraordinary efforts of the Federal Reserve and central banks around the world. Like the Tanker Air Carriers used to fight forest fires out west, the US Federal Reserve alone poured over a trillion dollars of liquid cash into the global banks around the world to prevent the crisis from shutting down all commerce. As we saw in March 2020, barely ten years after the 2008–2009 crisis, the underbrush returned, and lightning struck again, this time in the form of a pandemic and a shutdown for a period of months of virtually all economic activity. As we will discuss later in its response to this most recent crisis, the Fed has emptied their refilled tanks and appears once again to have put out the fire. To some of us, though, it seems to be a frighteningly close call. Once the underbrush returns and lightning strikes again, it is anybody's guess whether there will be enough water left in the storage tanks around the world to put out the next conflagration.

We still need to live in this uncertain, complex, and possibly fragile environment. It is beyond the scope of this book (and my expertise) to answer the question of how fragile the global economy is or what steps governments or others should take to minimize that fragility. However, the question that individuals and businesses need to face is what they can do to survive in this incomprehensibly complicated and overgrown financial forest.

I don't have any ready answer to this question either, but I think the metaphor of a forest fire is again instructive. As devastating as a forest fire can be, it will only consume the forest and other flammable material in the area. Furthermore, even when a macro-system in which you operate collapses around you, it doesn't necessarily destroy everything in it, and it may even be possible to find your way *out* of the system before you are destroyed. Consider, for example, whether the Columbia astronauts might have survived if there had been an escape hatch and a parachute or some other means to return to Earth available to them when their ship started to fail.

Individuals and businesses maintain all kinds of insurance, and many have other emergency preparedness plans, mostly to survive natural disasters like earthquakes and hurricanes. I would suggest that contingency planning and holding "non-flammable" assets like unleveraged real estate and physical commodities (e.g., food, fuel, gold) is one way to prepare for a financial forest fire that may temporarily require operating without money or other paper assets. Beyond "financial fire insurance," there are other ways to prepare yourself to survive if our financial system does, in fact, crash. We will talk about those in Chapter 8 when we discuss HFW Foundational Principle #5 and how to become antifragile.

I am not a survivalist, and some might find the likelihood of a financial system collapse highly unlikely. However, as Taleb points out, *"Our world is dominated by the extreme, the unknown, and the very improbable (improbable according our current knowledge)."*[21] Just like the centuries-old life insurance companies that are still in business, I believe that longevity is one of the best measures there is of effective risk management *and* an essential component to maintaining holistic financial wellness.

HFW Foundational Principle #1 means more than just being attentive to all the interconnectivity in your financial life. It also means being aware of the connections between your financial life and the bigger macro-system of money in which you operate. More importantly, awareness is the first critical step in being prepared for *all* the risks that might destroy you or your business, *including* the fragility of the environment in which you operate.

Chapter 2
Money and Debt—What Are They and Where Did They Come From?

"Take a look at this. Now *that* is an example of *real money*."
—Bob Y., FSA, showing a member of his team a rare, uncirculated nineteenth-century gold coin that he had just purchased.

Gold, Bubbles, and the Crash of '87

During my career, I've had the good fortune of working with some of the smartest actuaries in the country, and one of the brightest was my old boss, Bob Y. Bob graduated from Rutgers at the age of nineteen, quickly passed all his actuarial exams, and became one of the youngest FSAs in history (Oswald Jacoby, the famous Bridge master, actually holds the record, having become an FSA at age twenty-one). Bob started his career at Prudential Life Insurance but was soon recruited by Hewitt Associates. His ability to combine powerful mathematical thinking with a wicked sense of humor and a unique communication style that contained no extraneous information made him an extraordinary consultant.

At Hewitt, Bob quickly became the hero of all the young actuarial students in the office. Closer to our age than the other senior actuaries, he was approachable and funny, dressed even worse than us, with short-sleeved dress shirts, cheap loud ties, and suits that almost certainly came from some basement factory seconds sale. More than anything, though, he was fun and exciting to be around, both in and outside of the office.

While I'm sure the senior partners struggled to smooth his rough edges and contain his more impolitic outbursts (he was not shy about voicing his opinion on any subject, sensitive or not), clients loved him. His ability to take almost any actuarial problem and attack it with the power and focus (as well as the noise) of a pneumatic jackhammer made him an invaluable company asset that they guarded jealously.

I got to work directly with Bob when, in 1985, one of the firm's biggest clients moved to Southern California and asked Hewitt to make sure that Bob was available to continue working with them.

Bob adjusted to the new environment quite quickly, and with a bit more time on his hands (the laid-back SoCal approach to life infected even the actuaries of the area), he began to focus his curiosity on the (to his eyes) bizarre attitude toward money and "stuff" in general that permeated the culture. I distinctly remember the morning he arrived at the office and couldn't stop talking about the new front door that he and his wife had just put on their relatively new house in Lake Forest, one of the region's innumerable suburban subdivisions. All the houses in his neighborhood were almost identical, so a unique front door was perhaps more important there than the simple functional, sturdy requirements of doors that Bob was used to in New Jersey. But why, he asked, should such a door cost *$3,000!?* What exactly was the value proposition? Why was it so clear to his wife (who was also from New Jersey) that this was a necessary purchase, and why did his neighbors think that the price was not the least out of line? He was truly puzzled. The more he thought about it, the more he was convinced that this was a completely irrational price anomaly that was generated by a mass hallucination that could not persist forever. He believed that once the fever broke, the price of doors would plunge to more reasonable levels. This got him thinking that, while it was already too late to wait for door prices to revert to normal, there might be areas where some money could be made by taking advantage of the psychology of mass illusions in other parts of the market.

For the first time in his life, Bob had some money to invest, and with this investment strategy in mind, he began studying the history of price bubbles and the hysteria of crowds. Soon our morning conversations turned to the tulip mania of the seventeenth century[22] and the

South Sea Bubble one hundred years later.[23] At the same time, he began to read more carefully the *Wall Street Journal* and various investment market reports that came across his desk. After a few months, he believed that he had found a golden opportunity to bet against a price bubble that was inflating to the bursting point right before his eyes—the US stock market.

Throughout the 1980s, the Dow Industrial Index had been rising steadily, from around $750 in 1980 to over $2,000 in 1986.[24] This three-fold price rise made no logical sense to Bob, and when he looked more closely at individual stocks, he saw what looked like even more irrational behavior. Typical of Bob, however, he did not rush in and start selling stocks short. Rather, he began to investigate the mechanics of the market more closely, including the fast-developing world of derivative instruments (e.g., puts, calls, options), as well as other markets that he thought should bear some relationship to the price of US stocks. Included in these related markets were bonds, interest rate futures, commodities, and especially, gold.

Bob began to dip his toe in the water. Every morning, he would come in and talk about some new complicated investment play he'd discovered, or how combining two or more bets at the same time could produce either exponentially increased returns or provide a "guaranteed" return while hedging against some catastrophic market drop. In many ways, he was inventing the kind of quantitative analysis that in the 1990s and 2000s drove the growth of modern hedge funds that today employ hundreds of math and physics Ph.Ds. Of course, those "quants" also use more powerful super computers to do their analysis, while Bob did most of his number crunching with a Lotus spreadsheet running on a primitive IBM PC.

For a while, I was able to follow the intricacies of the new complex trades that Bob was contemplating, but soon it just became too abstract and unreal for me to see. How the money flowed, and who made what when one or another index changed (or even worse, when the spread between two different indices shrank or grew) simply lost all connection to the price of goods and services and what I thought of as "real" money. Even though I could no longer follow his thread, I was always interested to hear when he made a trade, which he began to do with increasing frequency.

In many ways, not only was Bob an early hedge fund quant, but he was also an early day trader, and while his eye was always on the big one (the ultimate stock market crash), which he saw as inevitable, he was able to supplement his income with some astute plays, taking advantage of "holes" and inefficiencies in the market. The main way he was going to make money when the market fell was through "out of the money" put options that he fully expected to fund his retirement when the cataclysm came. For those unfamiliar with the term, a put option is an agreement to sell a stock at a specific price before a specific date in the future. Theoretically, such options were supposed to be used to hedge against price drops of stocks that one already owned, but Bob was buying these as "naked puts," constituting a pure bet on a crash. The puts would be worthless if the stock market continued to rise or simply paused before the option expired (usually three to six months after purchase), but would make him extremely wealthy if there was a sudden and dramatic fall in the S&P 500 or Dow.

At the same time that Bob was making all these esoteric investments based on what he saw as the *illusion* of value in the stock market, he also began to dabble in a market where the reality of value was grounded in thousands of years of history; specifically, the gold market, and even more specifically, the market for rare gold coins.

This was 1986, and in his study of various bubbles, one that interested Bob had recently burst: the price of gold. Gold held a particular fascination for him because unlike the highly abstract investments he was making elsewhere, gold has historically been considered by humans as "real" money. I suspect that the idea of investing in something so tangible as gold in conjunction to his other, less concrete, holdings may have provided him a sense of ballast along with the diversification among different asset classes that conventional investment theory advises. Whatever the reason, Bob's investment portfolio began to look downright schizophrenic with his investments split between these two wildly different strategies. But as with almost every other venture he undertook, Bob had a thoroughly bulletproof rationale for each, and the dissonance between the two didn't seem to bother him one little bit.

To my mind, the rationale for the gold coin collection was quite compelling, and I was even persuaded to join the fun and buy some bullion myself. After the US went off the gold standard in 1973,[25] the price of gold began to be traded like any other commodity. The price initially rose (previously, it had been fixed at about forty dollars per ounce), but then seemed to stabilize at about $200 per ounce. Then in 1979 and 1980, gold became the hot investment to hold. Prices skyrocketed, hitting a peak of $850 in January 1980[26] before crashing back to more "normal" values. When Bob got interested in the market, the price was about $300, about one-third of the peak price it had hit six years earlier.

It was at this point that Bob started to accumulate gold. At first, he was interested in pure bullion, but very soon realized that if he was going to bet on gold as a true form of "money," he might as well go all the way and start buying gold coins. Soon he was attending coin shows all over Southern California and learning the intricacies of ascertaining the true condition of an allegedly "proof" or "uncirculated" coin. He befriended dealers, subscribed to numerous publications devoted to coin collection, and every Monday morning, he would regale me with the story of his latest weekend expedition and what kind of score he had made. One of the attorneys in our office characterized Bob and his fellow zealots as "monkeys picking up bits of shiny glass," but Bob was undeterred. Given his track record in the actuarial field, I certainly wasn't going to doubt him.

All through 1986 and most of 1987, Bob continued to pursue his unique "bimodal" asset allocation strategy. In a funny sort of way, both of his bets were coming from the same basic worldview—that much of what we think of as valuable dollar-denominated financial assets are merely figments of our collective imagination, held up by nothing more than a belief in the soundness of money, the measurement of value by experts, and faith in the future productive capacity of the American economy. In his view, that faith would ultimately prove illusionary; sooner or later, we would all realize this, leading the basic definition of money and value that had come about before the Roman Empire to reemerge.

While the apocalypse never arrived (though as I mentioned in the last chapter, it still might), on October 19, 1987 (Black Monday), the US stock market had its worst day in history, falling 22.6 percent in a matter of hours.[27] Unfortunately, as right as he was, Bob had not executed his strategy as precisely as he should have, and most of his "out of the money" puts had expired just days earlier. He told me later that many of his options would have been worth five hundred times the price he paid for them, had the crash happened just a couple of weeks before it actually did. Discouraged as he might have been, he felt vindicated that his basic analysis had been right. He continued to plow his remaining investable funds into rare coins. Meanwhile, the price of gold crept steadily upward, and people were willing to pay increasingly-higher premiums for actual coins as well. By the time I left the company in 1988, Bob's investment in "real" money was continuing to appreciate nicely, and he was already beginning to look into a new investment idea (racehorses) for his next big score. I wouldn't know exactly what form that investment would take until much later, but as I headed off to my next career stop, I took with me a vague but palpable unease that the money we use to calibrate our clients' liabilities, and the value of the investments that we say are backing those liabilities, is *far* less solid and measurable than we lead ourselves and our clients to believe.

In order to understand just how much of a house of cards our financial system has become, we need to go back in time and take a hard look at how money became what it is today.

A Brief History of Money and Debt

It turns out that money as we think of it today is a relatively recent development. Up until the late Middle Ages, money was simply a medium of exchange. It was a convenient, portable material—usually gold—that could be easily divided into portions that was measured out and used as a metric for determining the value of disparate goods and services. Fundamentally, money was a (brilliant) human technological invention created to facilitate the exchange of goods and services so that, for example, the butcher could exchange his meat for clothes without entering into a protracted barter negotiation with each customer. For thousands of years, this system worked well. The supply of gold was relatively constant, though of course, the discovery of new sources (or the conquest of others who possessed it) could instantly create wealth and was somewhat disruptive to the market. Nevertheless, by and large, everyone accepted the inherent value of gold.

People being people, however, society couldn't leave well enough alone, and in the 1500s, the business of banking was institutionalized. Two new and related "improvements" were incorporated into the system of money; specifically, the concepts of *debt money* and *interest*. These were formally adopted as natural phenomena that soon became inseparable from the idea of money itself. It is hard to overstate how important and controversial these two developments were at the time, although today it is almost impossible to imagine a world without them. While the concepts of both debt and interest arose much earlier in history, they were not woven into the fabric of our monetary system until the rise of commercial banking during the Renaissance.

The idea of interest came first, and its seeds were sown (literally) more than five thousand years ago during a time when the only industry in existence was the production of food, that is, agriculture and animal husbandry. People who needed to grow crops would obtain seeds from their neighbors, and once the crops were harvested, the neighbor would receive his seeds back as well as interest in the form of excess crops from the harvest. A similar approach was taken with respect to animals, whereby, for example, a bull was given to an individual who only had a cow, and after the two produced offspring, the bull was returned along with one of the newborn calves. As cities developed, a more complex economy emerged; with the use of metal money becoming prevalent, a new form of interest was invented. Specifically, instead of directly repaying the seeds or animals that were obtained with the bounty of the harvest (i.e., the organic growth of the commodity borrowed), interest could be charged and collected on money itself.

This was a remarkable conceptual leap and first occurred during the time of the pharaohs in ancient Egypt. As brilliant as this was, there were problems almost immediately. Beyond the philosophical issue of how a "sterile" material like gold could increase, the disconnect between the interest charged and the actual growth of the commodity being bought with the money borrowed created the heretofore unknown concept of "default." The ancients' approach to this problem was distinctly old-fashioned. If you couldn't pay the interest, you became a slave of the individual who provided the money in the first place. This gave rise to increasing social problems as more and more farmers became slaves to the money lenders. Aristotle himself argued strenuously against the concept of interest on money and was among the first to coin the term "usury."[28] For over a thousand years, the controversy over the morality of charging interest raged. All the major religions came down strongly against it (although in the Jewish tradition, individuals *are* allowed to charge interest to non-Jews), and in fact, even today, strict Islamic practice forbids the collection of interest.

Gradually, the concept of interest became accepted as long as there was some risk associated with the repayment of the money, and usury was redefined as interest in excess of what we now think of as the "risk-free rate of return" or what is often referred to as "the time value of money." Finally, in the early 1500s, usury itself was accepted as an inherent and necessary component of an increasingly complex economy where money flowed back and forth quickly and constantly between producers and consumers of goods and services. The time between the giving and receiving of money became long enough to need the concept of "the time value of money" to keep the system lubricated and operating efficiently. For those in the financial services industry, it is sobering to realize that one of the fundamental principles of finance, and one we rarely question (the time value of money) was, for more than a millennium, viewed as a serious evil in the world.

It's an interesting question to consider whether, without the rise of banks and the explosive growth of debt, the establishment of interest as a permanent feature of our monetary system would have been sustainable. Perhaps it would, but when the banks began to issue debt and change the very nature of money, the system began to go down a path that may eventually prove unsustainable. To understand why, we need to go back to sixteenth century England, where humble goldsmiths, the simple craftsmen who worked with the metal itself, invented the first fractional reserve banking system the world had ever seen.

For hundreds of years, goldsmiths had not only worked with gold—crafting, measuring, and trading it—but also, as a convenience for their clientele, *stored* it for those who didn't want to carry it around. For this service, they would provide their customer a receipt and charge a modest fee for the time the gold was in storage. It was a valuable service, and goldsmiths were very much trusted. So much so, that after a while, rather than use the actual gold, people were able to use the receipts that they had received from the goldsmith as money. In essence, goldsmiths had unintentionally entered the banking business.

Unfortunately, they didn't stop there. Like all businessmen, they looked for ways to increase their profits, and many of them realized that, because not everybody needed their gold at the same time, the goldsmiths were generally holding quite a bit of gold that could be utilized for other purposes. So, taking advantage of that fact, they started to loan out gold receip*ts* (i.e., money), to individuals who had no specific gold on deposit, knowing that even if the borrower "spent" the receipt with someone who would want to redeem it in gold, in almost all cases, the loan would be repaid (with interest) well before the receipt would be redeemed. In fact, if any of these newly issued receipts were submitted for redemption, they could use *other people's gold* to make good on their promise. Thus, at any one time, there might be five times as many receipts outstanding as actual gold to back them. It was a wonderful system that made goldsmithing a much more profitable business than it had been historically. The goldsmiths may not have found the philosopher's stone that could turn iron into gold, but they *had* found a way to create money out of nothing, or more specifically, to *create money out of debt*.

The only catch, of course, was what would happen if all the receipts were submitted at once. As times were relatively stable and financial disclosure rules were (at least for goldsmiths) non-existent, though, the situation continued like this for a surprisingly long time. As it turns out, it wasn't a "run on the goldsmiths" that ended the party, but rather the entrance into the game by some big players, specifically the banks themselves.

As far as I can tell, the first major bank to get into the business of issuing/creating money was the Bank of Amsterdam, founded in 1609.[29] At first, the bank adhered to very strict guidelines and only issued receipts (i.e., money) that were fully backed by gold on deposit. The safety, solidity, and reliability of this money soon became so attractive to the public that the bank grew substantially, and its money became the nearly standard currency used in the country. Other "central banks" started to emerge throughout Europe, and the use of paper money became ubiquitous. But the lesson of the goldsmiths was not lost on the banks. Soon, the ratio of actual gold on deposit to total money in circulation started to decline. Even the Bank of Amsterdam, founded on the principle of 100 percent reserving, started to create money by secretly making loans in excess of their gold reserves. Other banks were more transparent, and explicitly set reserve ratios at less than 100 percent. Business was good and the money supply magically grew as reserve ratios (both stated and unstated) fell. Eventually, the public accepted (or didn't think about) the fact that much of the money that they were spending didn't really exist at all but was simply created by banks issuing debt. As long as people were productive enough to pay back their loans with interest, the system worked.

For almost four hundred years (aside from the occasional bank panic), the system continued to work. I'm sure we've all seen George Bailey's eloquent defense of the fractional reserve banking system in *It's a Wonderful Life*.[30] I know I was taken in, and never really questioned the notion that banks would only hold a small percentage of their outstanding deposits in "real" assets. If you had asked me what that percentage was a few years ago, I probably would have said something like 25 percent. This notion, that 75 percent of all money is imaginary, conjured by banks by simply extending credit, should perhaps have been more disturbing to me than it was, since relying on our future productivity for 75 percent of our wealth does seem like a heavy burden. However, the situation is much worse than that.

I know we are no longer on the gold standard, and as we will discuss shortly, there are many brilliant economists and mathematicians who argue that our current system can endure indefinitely. But there is a simple ratio that worries me, and that is the comparison of the value of all the gold in the world to all the money in circulation. This ratio, of course, is not as simple to calculate as it sounds, but I took a shot. First, I asked the internet, "How much money is there in the world?" I got a lot of answers, as the way one defines money these days is understandably in some dispute. At the end of the day, using a very conservative measure (amount of checking accounts, savings accounts, and CDs, to name a few) it looked like $40 trillion (with $10 trillion in the US) was pretty much the consensus.[31] The value of all the gold reserves in the world was a little easier to determine, as it's a real thing that can be weighed and tracked. It turns out that there are about 34,000 tons of gold held by governments[32] and banks, among others, and at $1,300 per ounce, that works out to a bit more than $1 trillion worth of the metal. That gives a ratio of gold/money of a little under 3 percent.

More about Debt and Leverage

This degree of leverage is troubling enough, but the story does not end there. That 97 percent of money that we think we have but is actually debt is *in addition to the actual debt that we have explicitly taken on*, through mortgages and car loans, among others. Estimates of that amount are on the order of $200 trillion.

These days, debt comes in many forms, and most of us are both lenders *and* borrowers. In addition to the debt we have taken on via traditional car loans, mortgages, and credit cards, many of us are still saddled with student loans taken out for college or graduate school, as well as from hidden debt like car and rental leases that require us to pay back a fixed amount (or series of payments) in the future. Not only that, but most of us *own* debt as well, through the corporate and/or municipal bonds that we hold as investments in our savings and 401(k) accounts. Today, the world of debt is almost as complicated as the world of money itself, with a proliferation of different, yet often interrelated forms of borrowing available. Just consider the range of 15- and 30-year fixed and variable rate mortgages that are now available when you buy a house. Fortunately, as complicated as the different forms are, they can all be specified along a few mathematical/legal parameters.

Key Variables for Debt:

1. The duration of the loan: When in the future does the loan need to be paid back?
2. The interest rate accruing on the debt: This could be fixed or variable—a specified number or a floating "index."
3. The repayment terms: All in a lump sum, in periodic payments, or a combination.
4. Default provisions: What happens if the borrower doesn't pay the loan back?

While almost every form of debt can be described in terms of the above four parameters, there have been many financial innovations in lending (such as convertible bonds) that can affect its nature and can even change your investment from debt (i.e., bond) into equity (i.e., stock) under certain circumstances.

Throughout the rest of this book, we will talk about some of the dangers inherent in the modern complexities of debt, but the most important decisions that most people have to make throughout their financial lives is determining when to stay debt-free, when it is useful to take on debt, and when it is better to be a lender, reaping the investment returns by buying debt and counting on others to pay back what they have borrowed.

Debt is a double-edged sword, and while there are many who quite accurately describe its dangers and provide simple rules about avoiding it, decisions regarding debt are too complicated and idiosyncratic to boil down into a set of rules. To illustrate this point, I described earlier how the strategic use of debt and leverage allowed me to attain a modicum of financial security. Before we talk about when and how you can get in trouble by taking on debt, I want to share one more story about the downside of avoiding debt, or in this case, what can happen if you pay off what you owe too soon.

The Value of an Education

My friend Yaron is a very smart man. Son of Holocaust survivors, he emigrated from Israel in his mid-thirties after a short but successful career as a logistics officer in the Israeli army. Shortly after coming to the US, he fell in love with Sarah, a Harvard-educated emergency room physician who grew up poor but had recently been hired by a large Bay-area hospital system and whose future earnings prospects were very bright.

In short order, they got married and had two equally bright sons, both of whom Yaron quite willingly agreed to take care of while Sarah focused on securing their financial future. In addition to his child-rearing duties, Yaron also took on the task of making the strategic financial decisions in their lives. Now as I mentioned, Yaron was a logistics officer in his prior life, and as such, was skilled at deciding on "critical paths" and taking "first things first." To him, the first and most critical task facing their new family was to get rid of the almost $100,000 of student debt that Sarah had taken on to become a doctor.

Of course, there were other looming financial issues in their lives as well. There was housing and schools to consider, college tuition to save for, and, even further down the road, retirement security to think about. Unfortunately, like many of us, Yaron prioritized these issues in terms of the timing of the expense (student loans first, then housing and schools, followed by college savings and finally, retirement security). More importantly, he failed to consider the connections between the issues and consider his financial situation holistically.

And so, he and Sarah spent almost all their modest savings and extra disposable income from Sarah's practice paying off the student debt that seemed to be a dreadful financial and psychological burden to them. After five years of disciplined budgeting, they finally paid off the loan just as their oldest son was about to enter kindergarten. In a perfect world, they would have purchased a home in a nice neighborhood, but despite being debt-free, they did not have enough for a down payment and instead had to evaluate the trade-offs between high rent in a good school district or paying for a private school education. After extensive research on school districts and test scores, among other factors, Yaron and Sarah made the thoroughly rational (in isolation) decision to rent a small house in the section of town with the best public school system in the region and, once situated there, to save up for a down payment on a house in the same neighborhood (which, of course, had the highest house prices in the area).

Everything might have worked out, except the future is far more uncertain and unpredictable than we think. When they began paying off the loans, it was the late nineties and Yaron's assumptions as to what would happen to both the residential real estate market and the price of a college education were way off. In the next ten years, housing prices in Northern California (as well as the amount needed for a down payment) skyrocketed at rates not seen before or since. By 2007, when they finally accumulated enough to purchase a house, prices had risen well past the point of rationality. Yaron, quite rightly, decided that this was a bubble that he didn't want to participate in. Meanwhile, as this was going on, college tuition rates were increasing at double-digit rates. As Yaron thought about that looming problem, it seemed that paying for the kind of university his kids aspired to was something that would be even more difficult than owning their own home. Of course, these two issues are intimately related, and that was one of the key points that Yaron missed. Had he bought a house and taken on more debt instead of paying off Sarah's student loans, the leverage associated with owning an asset worth five times as much as the amount of upfront cash required would have allowed their home equity to grow (over the long-term) at a rate far greater than the increase in college costs (note that this is true even if year-to-year house price changes are volatile). Such a strategy would then have allowed them, over time, to both pay off the student loans and refinance their house to free up enough funds to pay

PETER NEUWIRTH, FSA, FCA

for college. In short, had Yaron and Sarah thought *holistically* about their situation, they would have been able to achieve all their financial goals.

Some may ask why I haven't talked about interest rates or taxes in telling Yaron and Sarah's story. The short answer is that it wouldn't change my message at all. In fact, had I done so, the availability of low-fixed rate mortgages and the tax subsidies inherent in home ownership would have made the case for buying a house instead of paying off their student loans even more compelling.

In retrospect, there was a small window of opportunity in 2010, after the financial crisis of 2008–2009, when Yaron and Sarah could have caught the housing market on the way back up and perhaps purchased a house whose future appreciation would have given them sufficient home equity to tap into (via a home equity line of credit) to finance their sons' education. But as many of us remember, those were frightening times, both for the markets and for the economy as a whole, and it was far from clear where house prices were headed.

In 2016, their oldest son graduated from high school, and this year, their other son will follow him into an uncertain future. Yaron and Sarah are facing an almost impossible financial situation that could have been avoided, not by timing the market via a 2010 house purchase, but rather by thinking holistically from the beginning, recognizing that assets and liabilities are both varied and connected, that not all debt is bad, and that almost all our current financial decisions have future consequences that, while not predictable, can be imagined and prepared for.

Where We Are Today

Positive as it may be on an individual basis to use debt and leverage to attain our financial goals, the truth is that all the debt that Americans have assumed has created a complex (and fragile) world. The sad fact is that in the last several decades, we have used our collective $40 trillion of nominal wealth as collateral to take on more debt and leverage ourselves further. Beyond that, in the last twenty years, we have seen banks, insurance companies (like AIG), hedge funds, and all kinds of other financial institutions develop increasingly complex and sophisticated ways to further increase the leverage under which they are operating (mostly through derivatives). A conservative estimate of the settlement value (the amount one party owes another) of these derivatives is over $700 trillion, with some estimates ranging over *$1 quadrillion(!)*.

A quadrillion is a bigger number than I ever expected to see with a dollar sign attached to it, and to my mind, it just underlines the unreality that surrounds the concept of money as it exists today. The whole thing seems like the scene from the movie *Fantasia*, where the sorcerer's apprentice conjures up a broom to clean up the wizard's lab and watches in horror as it magically makes copies of itself, at first increasing the speed with which the job gets done, but ultimately leading to chaos and catastrophe.

And yet, billions of us rely on money to survive, and the basic rationale for the existence of money as a medium of exchange is both valid and still critical to the functioning of the world. Happily, we are an adaptive species, and when I think about the future of money, I am actually pretty hopeful that we, and money itself, may evolve in ways that will enable us to continue and even thrive as the world around us gets more complicated and crowded every day.

I saw my old boss Bob one more time. It was shortly before the financial crisis of 2008–2009, and he was in great spirits, having just retired the year before (at age forty-nine) from Hewitt Associates. He had bought a racehorse and was planning on spending the next few years taking him from racetrack to racetrack around the country, hoping that he had found the next Secretariat. I asked him where his money was these days (knowing that no actuary, not even Bob, would rely on horseracing to provide a steady retirement income). His response was a simple, "Treasuries," and I knew immediately that his bet on the "true" value of gold, and rare coins in particular, had paid off in a big way. We didn't talk in any detail about his financial situation, but it was clear to me that before he retired, he must have done some reasonably detailed projections of his future income and expense streams and realized that the present value of the former exceeded the present value of the latter under all the scenarios he had considered.

How valid are those "present value" calculations when the money we measure does not represent real current value, but instead is 99 percent (or more) amounts that will be generated *in the future* to pay off the debt from which it was created? We have, it seems to me, a self-reference problem much along the lines discussed by Douglas Hofstadter in his book *Gödel, Escher, Bach: An Eternal Golden Braid*.[33] To equate the present to the future in terms of another quantity that is, itself, dependent on the future, is a logical paradox that has no obvious solution. Perhaps we should recalibrate our calculations to start with the 1 percent (to pick a number) of real value that exists, and then make some assumptions as to how the cash to be paid or received in future years relates to its expected (true) value at that time. However, that would require knowing, or at least guessing at, how the system of money will evolve in the future.

The actuarial profession's nominal expertise at developing future scenarios notwithstanding, I don't think anyone can know what will happen to money in the future. So much depends on what we *believe* money to be and what new technologies will be developed to either improve, or potentially degrade, the already shaky foundation on which the monetary system rests.

While the long-term future of money is unknowable, we *can* imagine some plausible scenarios. We now turn our attention to some developments happening *today* in the financial world, which, I suspect, will have a large impact on how our system evolves in the future. None of these new developments will reduce the complexity of our current system, but all have been developed with the best of intentions and may prevent, or at least forestall, any widespread collapse of our financial system that may occur in the future.

Chapter 3
The Future of Money and Debt

Bitcoin,ComplementaryCurrencies,andthePossibleDemise of Fiat Money

What the future of money holds is truly unpredictable (remember HFW Principle #4). However, there have recently been a few new developments that give me some hope. The first, and perhaps most important, is the emergence of alternative or complementary currencies that, while currently tiny, are being used to conduct a growing number of economic transactions. The most well-known of these new currencies is Bitcoin, but by focusing just on it, or even cryptocurrencies in general, we risk missing a much larger and maybe more significant picture.

Bitcoin: The New "Gold Standard"

About ten years ago, I went for a walk with my friend Eli, and he told me about a new technology that would forever change the way we think about money. Eli is a childhood friend and one of the smartest people I know. Our fathers were both theoretical mathematicians in Princeton, and while I became an actuary who worked with the practical issues associated with managing risk, Eli spent most of his adult life at Princeton, thinking about more abstract and theoretical matters. He worked as a particle physicist for many years before switching fields to computer science, where he soon became a leading artificial intelligence researcher at a large Japanese tech company and even wrote an important book on the subject.

By 2010, Eli had left academia and was living just up the road from me, enjoying the California lifestyle and trying to develop a computer system based on his theories of AI that would beat the best Go players in the world. At the time, many of his friends and colleagues considered it a quixotic venture that was impossible given the unimaginable complexity of the game, and in fact, he never succeeded. However, only a few years later, a team at Google developed AlphaGo, a learning program based on AI principles similar to Eli's that soundly defeated Lee Sedol, the world champion of Go, in a widely publicized match in 2016.

Eli has always focused his powerful intellect on problems of significance and scope, so when he said that there was something new, basic, and important happening in the financial world, I was ready to listen and try to understand.

As we started walking, Eli first described a famous, and heretofore unsolved, problem in information theory: "The Byzantine Generals Problem."[34] It was first posed in 1982 and concerned two or more Byzantine generals commanding separate armies seeking to conquer a city to incorporate it into their empire. The city in question has strong defenses and can only be conquered if the armies under the generals' command coordinate their attack to take place simultaneously and from opposite sides of the city. The problem is, how will the generals arrange to attack the city at the same time, given that any message they send to each other will have to be carried *through* the target city and be subject to sabotage? How can one general trust information received from another if it is transmitted through an insecure channel? More generally, this scenario demonstrates the problem users of a distributed network face when they must trust the information broadcast by one node of the network.

It took almost thirty years before the problem was finally solved by the invention of blockchain technology. Blockchain technology is now the current rage in the business world, and any company that purports to use it is automatically assumed to be cutting edge. Still, almost no one really understands how blockchain actually works. I know I don't. I understand that it involves the use of public registers, hashing, nonces, and some other technical computer science concepts, but why it is considered so earth-shattering is still a mystery to me. Eli, however, was extremely excited by this breakthrough, and in particular, the form of the solution to the Byzantine Generals Problem that had been developed by a guy named Satoshi Nakamoto. I tried to follow Eli's explanation, but I found myself getting lost in both the terminology and the complexity of the technical details. Finally, I asked him, somewhat impatiently, "But what does this have to do with money?"

Somewhat disappointed with my narrow intellectual bandwidth, Eli stopped his lecture on information theory and began to tell me about the new form of money that Nakamoto had invented using blockchain technology.[35] It was called "Bitcoin," and unlike dollars or gold, it was a form of money that *anyone* could create. All one needed was a fast computer and some software that would allow the individual to "mine" coins and put them in an "electronic wallet." Bitcoin, he said, would soon replace not just dollars, but all the various currencies now used throughout the world as a medium of exchange.

According to Eli, the reason Bitcoin was so superior to traditional currencies was because, unlike dollars, there was a fixed limit on how many bitcoins could be produced. And because it was not subject to central bank control (and manipulation), individuals would soon have greater trust in its use. The fact that it could be used for secret transactions that could not be traced by banks or governments would likely accelerate its acceptance among the multitudes of businesses and individuals who didn't want a public record of their transactions. The use of the new blockchain technology enabled this to occur and would also ensure that your possession of a legitimate bitcoin would be verifiable, but *how* you used it would not be disclosed to anyone except the parties involved in the transaction.

Essentially, Eli was saying that money itself had been reinvented; the fatal flaws now apparent in the current system of dollars (i.e., the almost unmeasurable supply of money and its disconnection with anything of real value like gold, as well as the control and power that banks had to "create" new money by simply issuing more debt) had been corrected. He believed that sooner than we imagined, we would be using Bitcoins to buy anything and everything, from pizzas and haircuts to everything in between.

Exciting as this all sounded, I was bothered by one thing. How, I wondered, were we going to get from a system where everything was denominated in dollars (albeit at values that may be illusory) to a system where Bitcoins were the medium of exchange? I understood that it was possible for some ordinary people to become Bitcoin miners, but how were the rest of us going to get these Bitcoins to spend? Eli was less than clear on how the ultimate transition to a Bitcoin-denominated economy might occur, but in the short term, he said that people would simply buy Bitcoins by exchanging their soon-to-be worthless dollars for this new currency. In fact, by the time we had our conversation, you could buy one Bitcoin for approximately eight dollars. Eli believed so strongly in the concept that he had bought 100 bitcoins and said he was going to hold on to them until the great transformation occurred.

You see, Eli had calculated that, given the enormous supply of dollars in the economy compared to the theoretical limit on the supply of Bitcoins, each Bitcoin should be worth about $1million. He figured that with a wallet of 100 Bitcoins, he would eventually be able to live as well in the future as the typical multi-millionaire today. Of course, the trick was that by the time his Bitcoins were worth $100 million, dollars themselves wouldn't be worth anything. Eli realized that if he were going to be wealthy man, at some point he would need to figure out how to convert his Bitcoins into something more tangible that *would* have value. While he hadn't solved that problem completely, he had decided to start spending his Bitcoins when they rose to $100,000 per coin and then gradually cash in the Bitcoins that he would never be able to spend for real assets (e.g., houses, art) that would be of lasting value.

As I say, Eli has one of the most powerful brains I have ever come across, but when I heard his vision of the future, I felt there was something he must be missing, and that the future of Bitcoin would not be nearly as clear as he was suggesting. I could not believe that just because Bitcoin was a better version of money, it would simply take over the role of dollars and other currencies. There was far too much inertia and entrenched power in the holders of the trillions of dollars that currently flowed through the system to enable a change of that magnitude from happening without a catastrophic disruption of our economy and the lives of billions of people around the globe. My bet was that it wouldn't happen.

It hasn't yet, and I am not sure it ever will, but Eli *had* figured out something important about our system that Bitcoin illuminated. The fact is that the leverage in the supply of dollars flowing around the world is real. The presence of Bitcoin, which has a limited supply and can be traded for dollars, made this fact dramatically apparent as the price of a Bitcoin exploded, rising to almost $50,000 per bitcoin in early 2021.[36]

Eventually, Eli recognized that the forces keeping the current system of money in place were too strong and that Bitcoin itself had some structural flaws that would prevent it from truly taking over our economy. So last year, he began disposing of his stash of Bitcoins, selling them well before they got to his $100,000 target. Even though he had given up on his vision of the future, his investment had paid off handsomely, and the compound annual rate of return on his $800 initial outlay was impressive indeed.

In *The Future of Money*,[37] Bernard Lietaer suggests that our current system of money is not sustainable and that, with the mountains of debt that underlie all money, we will essentially have to liquidate the Earth to pay off all that we owe to each other. He believes, in fact, that we are in the process of doing just that. His opinion is that the system will eventually crash, though when and how such a crash will manifest he does not profess to know. He does put forth several scenarios that seem highly plausible. Even though the crash he envisions could be very disruptive, some of those future scenarios are not as bad as they might seem, mostly due to the development of "complementary currencies"[38] that do not rely on either debt or interest for their existence. Instead, these new currencies are designed for the sole purpose of serving money's historical function as a medium of exchange. Unlike Bitcoin, these currencies operate in a limited geography or sector of the economy. Lietaer believes that their existence may cushion the blow when either dollars (along with euros, yuan, and pesos, among others) all become valueless or when big institutions like banks and countries begin to default and stop paying *their* debts.

The entire rationale for the development of Bitcoin was exactly this—to create an alternative currency that would serve as a trusted medium of exchange. It would have a finite and known supply, whose growth would be constrained and never be subject to the "money creation magic" that banks perform by issuing debt, which has inexorably led to the situation we just described.

Unfortunately, somewhere along the way, Bitcoin became something not quite as pure as its original intent. While I am not an expert, I believe the fundamental reason is that Bitcoin and other cryptocurrencies became too easy to exchange for dollars. Once that happened, Bitcoin became less of an alternative currency and simply *another* currency. But what kind of currency is it and why is it worth $50,000 per Bitcoin? Well, one reason for the lofty price might be that Bitcoin investors are just making a bet that dollars will go away, and the price of Bitcoin reflects the market's judgment that there is a one in twenty chance of the demise of dollars (.05 x $1 million = $50,000). I think, though, that the reason may be a little more straightforward and is related to one of the ways that Bitcoin is used (vs stored as an investment) today—that is, to conduct transactions that are not discoverable by others.

As a "foreign currency," Bitcoin has the unique capability, due to blockchain technology, of being used for secret and secure transactions. Cash dollars also have this ability, but hundred dollar bills can be traced, and if you are conducting a huge illicit transaction, carrying that much cash can be awkward. Besides, as we will see below, cash itself is disappearing, and before too long, the only material money you see will be in flea markets and antique stores. Bitcoin (and other cryptocurrencies) are in some ways ideal for transacting business in the "underground" economy. My view is that Bitcoin has become the de facto currency for the "country" that represents all "hidden" activities conducted throughout the world. Assuming that is the case, the key question, then, is how big is that economy, and how reasonable is the value of Bitcoin, given its limited supply relative to the magnitude of the goods and services that are bought and sold with it? To me, $50,000 seems like a pretty reasonable number. From that perspective, even at $50,000 per coin, it might still be a good investment, even if dollars never go away as the dominant currency used throughout the world.

Fundamentally, I think Bitcoin was a noble experiment that failed in its original intent to put the world of money back on sane and solid footing. That's not to say that Bitcoin or some other cryptocurrency won't ultimately replace dollars as the money that a lot of the world uses to transact business; in fact, by doing so, we may reduce some of the leverage in the current system. But, like many other good ideas, Bitcoin has become something different than its idealistic inventor envisioned. It is not what Lietaer or I mean when we talk about complementary currencies.

Right now, there are over five thousand separate complementary currencies being used to buy and sell things. Some are global and very familiar to all of us, like frequent flyer miles, which can be used on various sites to exchange for other goods and services. Others are local, community-based, and virtually unknown outside of where they can be used. These currencies are fundamentally different from Bitcoin in that, while they may have been acquired by buying them with dollars, as a general rule, there are barriers to converting them *back* into dollars. In other words, they are not a "hedge" or an investment. Instead, they are designed to be used strictly to exchange one good or service for another.

BerkShares, Ithaca Hours, and Buying Local

Sometimes, as in the case of frequent flyer miles, the goods and services that can be purchased with an alternative currency are very limited, but the geographical and demographic extent of their use is very broad. There are other complementary currencies that are not designed to profit a given company, but rather to serve a specific community. These seem to me to be much more socially good and less likely to be absorbed into the current monetary system. It is these currencies that could provide us shelter and sustenance if a financial forest fire along the lines we described in Chapter 1 actually occurred. These currencies allow for a broad array of goods and services to be exchanged, operating independently from dollars and in a geographically limited region. The two main types are community-based currencies and time-based currencies.

Community-based currencies are currencies that are local in nature and can only be used to purchase goods and services in a well-defined community. One example that has been particularly successful is BerkShares, which operates in Berkshire County, Massachusetts.[39]

You can acquire BerkShares by buying them with dollars from sixteen community banks that have contracted with the county and local businesses to be the creator and recordkeeper for the money. Even though businesses in distress with excess BerkShares are allowed to redeem them for dollars (at a steep discount), there is no market for it. The presumption is that they will stay in circulation as long as the community exists. More BerkShares are issued and sold by the community as more people and businesses join. Supply growth does need to be managed, but since no interest is paid on BerkShares that are saved and no debt is issued, the issues associated with the unsustainable leverage in the dollar system don't exist. The system has been in place since 2006, and there are currently about $7 million in BerkShares in circulation.

Time-based currencies share many attributes with community-based currencies, but have two additional features that could make them potentially more widespread in the future. One example is Ithaca Hours,[40] which started in Ithaca, NY, just a few miles west of Berkshire. They operate like BerkShares, and have been around longer, but in addition to obtaining Ithaca Hours by buying them with dollars, one can earn Hours by contributing actual time in the form of performing services for the "bank" that issues the currency (in this case, a not-for-profit organization in Ithaca in collaboration with a local credit union). Of course, a person can also earn Hours by providing a service to a community member who would then pay for it in Hours, but in the case of Ithaca Hours, the connection to time is made explicit. In some sense, it provides a useful benchmark for managing the growth in the supply of the currency. In other words, as was the case when money was invented, the currency itself is pegged to something that everyone considers valuable (i.e., time vs. gold). By using a "time standard" instead of a gold standard, time-based currencies are also somewhat more scalable and geographically unconstrained, since time is something everyone has no matter where they live. In fact, there is now a Global Time Exchange[41] that allows services to be exchanged internationally.

No one knows how far and wide these types of currencies will spread and proliferate, but in my view, complementary currencies of both types may represent our best hope for the future. To understand why, we need to return to Nassim Taleb's concept of antifragility.

One of the key principles in making systems not just resilient, but antifragile, is that to the extent possible, the system should *not* be too big, too uniform, or subject to centralized control. Rather, the most stable systems are those that are not organized in a hierarchical or even "hub and spoke" manner, but are instead highly dispersed and diverse. In such a system, a failure of one part will not bring down the other parts, and may, in fact, strengthen the system as a whole by creating space for other parts of the system to grow.

To understand this, let's start with a thought experiment. Suppose Bitcoin does succeed in taking over from dollars as the medium through which we conduct our economic life. The question then becomes: Would the system really be more stable? Yes, it's true that the flaws in the current system of money would be cured, but there would still be only *one* kind of money in circulation. Even if Bitcoin could be converted into another cryptocurrency (the way you can exchange pesos for Swiss francs), the system itself could still be brought down in the same way that the financial crisis of 2008–2009 almost brought down the global economy despite the multitude of traditional currencies that were in existence.

One of the principles of resilience (and ideally, antifragility) is that the system should be impervious or even get stronger when subjected to stress. Certainly, a system based on Bitcoin or another cryptocurrency would not be subject to the same kind of stresses that defaults on subprime mortgages created in the overleveraged opaque dollar-denominated economy of 2008, but are there other stresses, including ones we can't yet imagine, that might disrupt a Bitcoin economy? How about malicious hackers, technological glitches, power outages, or other hazards that might plague a fully digital decentralized currency? We just don't know.

Just like the many other ecosystems, natural and otherwise, true stability and antifragility come from not just diversity, but *uncorrelated* diversity. I believe we need *many varieties* of money that operate independently and are not so easily transferrable from one into another.

Taleb describes many types of diversified decentralized systems that are antifragile, including political systems (which, when you think of it, are not so dissimilar in complexity and structure to our financial system). He makes the compelling case that the city state system is far more stable than the large powerful centralized governments that have evolved. As he points out, Switzerland, which has no central government, but is instead a loose confederation of semi-independent Cantons, has been the most stable country in the world over the last one thousand years.[42] Loose confederations of Native American tribes that inhabited the western United States between 800–1600 (e.g., the many different tribes of Pomo Indians in Northern California)[43] are another good example of stable sustainable political systems.

Whether we can smoothly transition to such a decentralized approach to our financial system is a very important question. The fact, however, that complementary currencies exist and are growing suggests that the future is not nearly as apocalyptic as might appear from the current state of the world of money.

That being said, it may very well be that our current system of money will, through the heroic efforts of the Federal Reserve, survive. Ever since the US abandoned the gold standard in 1971, the Fed has been tasked with keeping our system of money running smoothly and avoiding the kind of catastrophic collapse that complex systems are prone to. In the section below, we will talk about how the Fed came about, how it does its job, and what its prospects are for future success in keeping this complex and fragile system up and running. For your purposes, it is important to remember that in order to survive a financial forest fire, it is not absolutely necessary to know how firefighters do their job, but knowing what resources the fire department has and how they deploy those resources to contain and put out the fires can be helpful as you think about where to put your financial assets to keep them from going up in smoke when the next financial crisis hits.

Dematerialized Money, Negative Interest Rates, MMT, and the Viability of Fiat Currency

In the spring of 2019, well before COVID-19 rendered air travel a dangerous activity, I dropped my twenty-year-old son off at Oakland Airport. He was flying to New York, where he would be moving into a new apartment in the city and getting ready to start his summer internship at a big corporation in Manhattan. He had flight connections to make, taxis to catch, baggage and furniture to move in, and a slew of other complicated logistical tasks ahead of him.

As we said goodbye, I asked him how much cash he had in his wallet and if he needed any extra in case of emergency. He gave me a look of bemused kindness—the kind you give a small child who wonders how the actors got so small that they could fit inside the TV. He not only had no paper money (or even a credit card) in his pocket, but he wouldn't even humor me by taking a few twenties to keep me from worrying about him. He explained to me that money in the way I thought of it was not part of his world. He had his smartphone, his Venmo and PayPal accounts, as well as a driver's license and passport to prove he was who he said he was if there was some technological failure with his phone.

Of course, cash is still an important part of my life and that of billions of people around the world, but it is clear that the dematerialization of money is well under way. It won't be too many years before my son's approach to money will be the norm.

The trend away from material money has been going on for hundreds of years, but in the last few decades it has accelerated dramatically, and the implications of this phenomenon are well worth considering. In a sense, the trend started almost five hundred years ago, when the goldsmiths began issuing IOUs for the gold that they safeguarded. These IOUs were much easier to carry around than the physical gold (i.e., real money) that they represented. It seems that that has been the motivation that has driven this trend—physical convenience. From banknotes to checkbooks to credit cards and now to Venmo accounts that are accessed by our smartphones, we have sought to distance our bodies from the physical reality of money. There may even be psychological, as well as economic, reasons for this as many people (and cultures like the French) consider money as dirty and don't want to touch it. However, the dematerialization of money has also had effects on our economy, and with the complete disappearance of cash, I believe we will see even more dramatic impacts.

Thus far, the impact of dematerialization has been to increase the speed and efficiency by which money moves from one party to another, particularly for large financial transactions. Imagine, if you will, the time and energy it would have taken in the 1700s to complete the purchase of a large house. The buyer would need to withdraw his or her funds from their bank and actually give it to the seller who would then need to transfer the money and redeposit it in their bank. The seller might want actual gold to be sure that the money was real. In addition to the delays and effort involved in conducting the actual transaction, the parties would also need to be concerned with the safety of having that much gold in their possession, even for the relatively brief time during which the actual exchange took place. These days, funds move much more quickly and securely between buyers and sellers. That is mostly a good thing and, in fact, is the essential reason money was invented: to facilitate the exchange of goods and services.

The speed and efficiency have, however, led to some unintended consequences that aren't so positive. Because money now moves at the speed of light, it is often hard for ordinary people to keep track of it. Banks and other financial institutions take advantage of the time lags and the "float" (i.e., the time between when the buyer lets go of their money and when the seller expects to receive it) by using the money in the days, hours, and even seconds when they have possession of the funds. I believe that many of the innovative financial instruments and technologies that have so complicated our system were developed as a result of this transformation of money from paper to electrons. Opacity and human greed have not helped matters.

The question I want to turn to now is what will happen when physical money disappears entirely? In fact, while the disappearance of physical money may make the system even more complex and fragile in the future, I also think, paradoxically, that this phenomenon will allow the "managers" of that system to keep it from crashing. Doing so could give us enough time for a more sustainable system to emerge. The key to this will be *negative interest rates.*

In order to become an actuary, I had to pass a series of exams that dealt with a range of subjects central to actuarial science. One of the early and fundamental ones was on "The Theory of Interest." The math was interesting, and I soon became adept at manipulating and solving problems that focused on all sorts of financial instruments including bonds, annuities, sinking funds, and many other esoteric forms of financial machinery. Interest could be paid annually, monthly, daily, and even continuously, but it could never be negative. The idea of an interest rate below zero was never considered in any of my study material, not even from a theoretical perspective. And with good reason: it made no sense. If some bank was crazy enough to tell its depositors that it would credit a negative interest rate (i.e., charge the customer for keeping their money in the bank) the bank would soon have no customers, as everyone would withdraw their money and keep it in cash.

But what if cash no longer existed? What if the *only* place money existed was in the digital records kept at the bank or other financial institution holding funds? Wouldn't it then be possible for interest rates to go below zero, both for interest credited on accounts and interest charged on loans outstanding?

The above question may seem wildly unrealistic and something that could only occur in a scary episode of *Black Mirror*, but it's not. Not only is it possible, it is happening today—not yet for ordinary depositors and borrowers like you and me, but for big banks and institutional investors in Europe and Japan, for whom holding stacks of billions of paper euros or yen is not a practicality. In countries where this is occurring, no one is getting upset. In fact, the ability of central banks to push interest rates into negative territory is viewed by and large as a great thing, perhaps the one thing that will save our system from collapsing—at least for a while. To understand why this is true, we need to review the role that central banks play in the financial system and see why it is so important that they have this power.

The central bank that is most familiar to you is probably the US Federal Reserve, or the Fed. In some ways, the Chairman of the Fed is the most powerful person in the US. The first chairman was appointed in 1914 by President Woodrow Wilson, shortly after the Fed was created by Congress in 1913. In its 105 years of existence, there have been fifteen chairman and one chairwoman—Janet Yellin, who was appointed by President Barack Obama. Jerome Powell is the current chair. When he speaks, vast numbers of journalists and financial professionals analyze every single word and phrase, not just for what they mean, but for what they imply. Whole markets can shudder or soar based on what those who control big money believe the Fed will or will not do the next time they meet.

In some ways, you can think of the Fed as the bank of the banks. It is where almost all banks in the US do their banking. It is also where the US government keeps its money and from which it pays its bills. In fact, in order to even start a (big) bank, you need to get approval from the Fed and then set up a reserve account there. This reserve account is funded with US Treasury Bills that the bank must buy with its original capital.

Like other ordinary banks, the Fed takes in money, holds assets, and keeps track of its depositors' accounts. For example, the government deposits all its tax receipts and other revenue that it generates at the Fed and pays its bills with checks from accounts held there. Even more importantly, like any other bank, the Fed lends money—mostly to other banks.

It also has another, almost magical power that other banks don't have. You see, the Fed can literally print money. In fact, all the paper money you have in your pocket are "Federal Reserve Notes." This cash comes from the Fed and is distributed to any bank that asks for it. In return, the bank has its reserve account with the Fed debited.

Why are banks allowed to just order up stacks of hundred dollar bills any time they want? Well, in order to be authorized by the Fed to get the cash, a bank needs to prove that it has sufficient capital to meet the reserve requirements that the Fed sets. This capital may come from the initial investment that the bank founders make when the bank is formed, or from assets that have been accumulated since the bank opened for business. The fact that that capital likely comes from money that is held at *another* bank is a paradox worth contemplating, but in the end, it is really just a manifestation of the ephemeral and faith-based nature of our money system. Nevertheless, despite the paradox, the value of the capital itself is tangible and can even be in the form of real estate or company stock, which represents the value of future earnings, something that we can agree on is real.

Once a bank is in business and operating, the Fed does two more things that are of critical importance. First, they determine the minimum amount of reserve that a bank must maintain, and second, they manage the key interest rates that banks pay and receive on deposits (which is why you often read about the fear or hope that "the Fed will raise rates").

The minimum reserve requirements directly affect the extent to which banks can create money by issuing debt. This is the fractional reserve banking that goldsmiths invented 500 years ago, and which George Bailey explained in *It's a Wonderful Life*. It is the reason that over 99 percent of the money in the world doesn't really exist, but is simply fiat money based on nothing more than our faith that we will be able to produce things with enough value to pay off all the debt that is backing that money.

The main way the Fed controls interest rates is by setting the rate that banks must pay if they want to borrow more money to increase their reserves to the mandated minimum. Banks need to do this periodically to be able to grow their loans and generate profits. Issuing loans is the main way banks make profits, and it is one of the main engines of our economy. If the Fed sets this interest rate too high, then the banks will stop lending out money and therefore slow down the economy. Conversely, when the Fed reduces these interest rates, the economy speeds up. While I have oversimplified this story a bit, raising and lowering interest rates is the main way that the Fed and other central banks seek to manage the economy to avoid the boom-and-bust cycles that had historically plagued the world when money was directly backed by gold.

Historically, the Fed has generally done a good job of keeping the system on an even keel, but during the financial crisis of 2008–2009, it was only barely able to keep the system from crashing completely. With the economy in free fall due to the collapse of the real estate market, mortgage-backed securities defaulting, and a long series of corporate dominoes (e.g., AIG) beginning to fall, the Fed desperately needed people to keep spending money and banks to keep lending money to keep the system functioning. As a result, they dropped interest rates to virtually zero, which was as low as they could theoretically go. In addition, they reduced reserve requirements and started buying up many of the defaulting loans from the banks themselves (the "toxic assets" that we heard so much about). They not only used all the familiar levers they had at their disposal, but Ben Bernanke (who was the Fed Chairman at the time) took the unprecedented step of using the Fed's own assets (as the biggest bank in the world) to try and stop the bleeding. They were successful, but it was a near thing.

Although the Fed was able to save our system again during the economic crash caused by COVID-19 (with some additional tricks we will talk about shortly), next time we might not be so lucky. That is, unless the Fed can push interest rates *below zero*, and this is where the full dematerialization of money is required. Once money only resides in the digital records of banks and cash no longer exists, then there is no theoretical limit as to how low interest rates can go. To put it in perspective, history has shown that to pull the economy out of a typical recession, the Fed needs to lower interest rates by 3 to 6 percent. In May 2008, when it was obvious that a crisis was incoming, the Fed's discount rate (the rate at which banks could borrow from the Fed) stood at 1.98 percent. They simply didn't have the room they needed to stop the fall. That is why the Fed had to resort to extraordinary measures to pull the economy back from the brink. The next time a crisis of this magnitude occurs, and rates are at that level, don't be surprised if you see the discount rate dropping to as low as negative 4 percent or lower. Think about your own money. No matter how bad the business environment looks, wouldn't you borrow and invest money if the bank would *pay* you to do so?

If you still think that the above is just wild speculation, consider this recent post from a staff member of the International Monetary Fund

(IMF), which oversees the international monetary system and monitors the financial and economic policies of 189 countries:

> *In a cashless world, there would be no lower bound on interest rates. A central bank could reduce the policy rate from, say, 2 percent to minus 4 percent to counter a severe recession. The interest rate cut would transmit to bank deposits, loans, and bonds. Without cash, depositors would have to pay the negative interest rate to keep their money with the bank, making consumption and investment more attractive. This would jolt lending, boost demand, and stimulate the economy.*[44]

So how should we prepare for this strange future where alternative forms of money proliferate and interest rates on our savings can go below zero?

As we said in Chapter 1, you can think of our financial system as a tangled, overgrown forest where it is easy to get lost, hard to make your way out of, and where huge wildfires can rage without warning.

As we suggested, having some insurance in the form of nonflammable assets like unleveraged real estate and other real property is prudent, but being psychologically prepared for this new world may be even more important. Consider looking for a community near you that has one of the complementary currencies discussed earlier and actively participate. Think of it as moving some of your financial life out of the forest and up the mountain to a spot above the tree line where you can stay safe in the event of a forest fire. In addition to being fun, you can be part of the movement that may very well be the path to a sustainable economy. If the economy does crash, you may find that your BerkShares or Ithaca Hours are far more valuable than you ever thought possible.

In the meantime, when the next financial crisis comes and you suddenly find that your bank is charging you to keep your money, don't panic or get mad. Just understand that it's only the firebombers overhead dropping high-tech fire retardant on the flames to save the economy.

Before we leave the subject of how money works, we should give due credit to how well the Fed performed during the Spring of 2020 when it was not at all clear that simply filling the country's bank vaults with newly printed dollars would save the day. In fact, during the COVID-19 crisis, the Fed not only created trillions of dollars to fund the banks, but they went further. They used their power to buy trillions of dollars' worth of corporate and municipal bonds—forms of debt that, with a crashing economy, could easily have defaulted and brought all commercial activity to an abrupt and catastrophic halt. At the time, it may have seemed like a reckless gamble with the stability and value of money itself, but a new economic theory called Modern Monetary Theory (MMT)[45] provided policymakers some hope that it would work. A discussion of the details of MMT is well beyond the scope of this book, but for readers who are interested, Stephanie Kelton's book, *The Deficit Myth*,[46] provides a very readable discussion of how and why it works. For our purposes, it is only important to know that these days, the Fed is prepared to go much further than they have previously gone before to create enough money to keep the system running. Let's hope that they and Ms. Kelton are right. That being said, I, for one, plan on buying a few Bitcoins and other non-flammable currencies in case they are wrong.

Getting Help—It's a Noisy World

Chapter 4
The Danger of Good Intentions

"The average family exists only on paper and its average budget is a fiction, invented by statisticians for the convenience of statisticians."—Sylvia Porter[47]

It turns out that even though men now dominate the world of personal finance and investment advising, it was actually a woman who invented the profession of financial planning. In the 1930s, Sylvia Porter began writing a personal financial advice column for the *NY Post* called "S.F. Porter Says." As has been the case too often in history, no one knew Porter was a woman until 1942, well after the column had become too popular and well established for anyone to care about her gender.

In a story that echoes those of many of the current providers of financial advice, Porter started writing about financial matters as a result of a financial calamity. Like many at the time, her family had lost much of their money in the Wall Street Crash of 1929. Porter was more fortunate than others in that this setback did not completely destroy her financial future, but it did instill in her a burning desire to help as many people as possible to avoid her fate. Unlike many of those who came after, Porter was both authentic and knew what she was talking about. Graduating Magna Cum Laude from Hunter College in 1932, she applied her brilliant mind to a relentless study of the financial world, quickly picking up an MBA from NYU while simultaneously working for the investment firm of Glass and Krey. By the time she reached her mid-twenties, Porter's fluency in the bond, gold, and foreign currency markets rivaled that of her most accomplished male colleagues.

Porter was unlike the current crop of financial advisors in other ways as well. By all accounts, her ethics were of the highest caliber and she was passionate about educating the general public on financial matters. She was one of the first people to see the growing complexity and opacity of our financial system as a threat to the financial well-being of the working class. She called the way financial matters were communicated "bafflegab," and it was her mission to educate the public as best she could. She fought tirelessly to protect consumers against banks and other financial institutions that took advantage of ordinary working people's ignorance and misplaced trust in those who controlled both the supply and flow of money.

Porter's column and the books that she began writing in the late thirties generated an enormous following. Soon, many other papers and magazines started to feature financial advice columns. In the economic boom that began after World War II, the financial world itself grew dramatically, both in size and in complexity. Unfortunately, the dramatically increased demand for financial advice attracted other less idealistic players to the field.

Please don't misunderstand me. I am not saying that there aren't honest, intelligent, and well-meaning individuals in the personal finance and investment advising industry. There are many, but the field is now overcrowded. More importantly, as money and investment markets have become overwhelmingly complex, the line between the provision of advice and the sale of "product" has blurred, and anyone who is not an expert in the field will struggle mightily to determine when they are getting independent, let alone useful, advice.

The detailed history and development of the personal finance and advising industry is an interesting topic, but not one that is the focus of this book. Instead, I want now to dig more deeply into who is giving advice today and what they are saying, and equip you with the tools you need to understand the advice you hear from the those who write books and fill the internet with their opinions and prescriptions. I want to help you identify the false notes you will hear in the sweet songs they sing and to avoid the dangers entailed in blindly following their instructions. In the next few pages, we will survey the landscape, discuss some of the more prominent players in the field, and highlight where many of the dangers lie. We will start with someone who almost everyone is familiar with and who, in many ways, illustrates how we got to the current state of affairs and what you need to be careful of as you try to maintain your financial health.

Comfort Food and Suze Orman

In the late nineties, my partner and I ran a small actuarial consulting firm in Berkeley, California. Because we specialized in defined benefit pension plans and most of our competitors were large and full-service, we were constantly on the lookout for other small consulting firms with whom we could form strategic alliances to fill in the gaps in our offerings. In particular, because most companies that had a pension plan at that time also had a 401(k) plan, we were in need of a firm that could provide expert advice on the design and administration of defined contribution programs like Profit Sharing and 401(k) plans. Fortunately, just down the road in Emeryville was a small firm structured just like ours that specialized in such plans. Its two founders, Leif and Brian, were topnotch retirement plan consultants who had spent nearly a decade working for large national employee benefit consulting firms.

Serendipitously, Leif and Brian were themselves looking for a company like ours to partner with, and so we set up a meeting to explore the possibilities of working together. Unlike our firm, which had a fairly mundane origin story, Leif and Brian's firm was born out of a dramatic middle-of-the-night breakaway from Watson Wyatt (a company I used to work for), complete with intrigue, stolen clients, threatened lawsuits, and a full range of drama. In spite of, or maybe because of, its tumultuous beginnings, their firm was almost immediately successful. Leif and Brian were nothing if not risk takers, and in just over three years, their bets paid off and they had grown their business dramatically. By the time we met, they had outgrown their original modest location and just moved into a space near the top of one of the tallest buildings in the Bay area with a spectacular view of the San Francisco skyline. After lunch they invited us back to their offices to take in their unique four-bridge view and discuss ways that we might jointly market our services. Situated in their large conference room, they talked about the many clients they had acquired since their founding and all the players in the retirement services world that they knew and could introduce us to. During the conversation, Leif casually mentioned that he had recently had a meeting with Suze Orman. My partner and I were both impressed.

"Do you really know Suze Orman?" I asked.

"Absolutely, she actually now has a small staff and we talked with her about her own company's situation," Brian replied with some pride.

"That's pretty impressive," I said. "It must be interesting working with someone so knowledgeable about our business."

At this point there was silence. Brian looked at Leif, and Leif looked at Brian. Then they both gave me a look that I can only describe as cryptic. Finally, Leif said carefully, "Suze is a *very* nice person. We liked her a lot."

Now, up until that time, I hadn't really paid much attention to Suze Orman. By then she had become fairly famous in the Bay area but was not the national icon she is today. I had heard snippets of her local radio show and found her advice sensible, but mind-numbingly obvious (e.g., "Pay off the credit card, and DON'T buy that boat!"). I didn't know any of her backstory, and I had assumed that she was just a fairly sophisticated financial practitioner who needed to dumb down her advice to reach her listeners. However, Leif's comment gave me serious pause and provided me with my first introduction into the world of financial planning. It was the first of many disillusionments I was to suffer about what financial planners like Orman base their advice on and the value of what they have to say.

In the twenty years since that conversation, I have watched with increasing alarm as more and more Suze Ormans have come on the scene and their advice has become louder, more strident, and in my opinion, more wrong. Worse than wrong; much of it is given by individuals who are hopelessly conflicted. In other words, they do *not* have their listener/

reader's best interest at heart, and as a result, following their suggestions can even be *dangerous* to one's financial health.

I don't think Orman gives bad advice—at least she didn't in the beginning of her career. Until fairly recently, I found most of her advice to be reasonable and given with the sincere desire to help her audience. Unfortunately, like almost everyone else you read or listen to, there is much more to what she says than meets the eye.

Orman's story is now well-documented, downright inspirational, and in many ways, similar to Sylvia Porter's. I start with Orman because I believe her success, along with that of a few other "early entries" has led to a "race to the bottom" in terms of the quality and usefulness of the bulk of the personal financial advice that is now generally available. But let's go back to Orman and her rise from a minimum wage job at a local breakfast place to the extremely wealthy self-made woman of influence she is today.

There is no debate about the loyalty and affection of Orman's customers at The Buttercup Bakery and how they lent her $52,000 to open her own restaurant or about her experience of losing that entire amount through the bad investment advice given to her by an unscrupulous/incompetent broker at Merrill Lynch. It is also clear that she used that setback as a motivation to become an investment advisor herself, earning back her original investment many times over and then embarking on a mission that she continues to this day; that is, to help people avoid financial disasters like the one that befell her. Unlike many in the business, by all accounts, Orman *is*, as Leif said, "a very nice person," and she *has* helped a lot of people.

But there is a dark side to the Suze Orman story that is less well known. Let's start with her actual financial acumen. In *Pound Foolish*,[48] a wonderful, if slightly overly simplified, critique of the financial planning industry's failure to disclose conflicts of interest and serve the public's interest, author Helaine Olen describes Orman's rise as a financial advisor, highlighting her unique talent for empathy and sales in contrast to her lack of real understanding or talent for the substance of the field. Olen quotes one of Orman's managers as saying that there were much better investors, but "no one who could market to investors better" than she could.

This impression was validated by the fact that almost all of Orman's considerable personal wealth can be traced to her prodigious book sales (rather than successful investing) and her own admission that she does not follow her own advice when it comes to investments. As Olen notes, Orman puts most of her money into ultra-safe municipal bonds rather than the stock market, while she is on record as advising her audience to invest so that they can receive the "normal stock returns of 11 to 12 percent per year." Even as late as 2012, Orman was recommending investing in stocks, referring her audience to a market timing investment newsletter (the "Money Navigator") that she explicitly endorsed.[49] Beyond being somewhat hypocritical, it was pretty clear that Orman has neither the theoretical grounding nor the practical experience to make tactical market timing decisions, let alone hold herself out as an expert in such matters.

Unfortunately, it gets worse than that. Because Orman has been in business for long enough for her predictions (e.g., "normal stock returns of 11 to 12 percent") to be proven embarrassingly false, she is now in a position to give advice that directly contradicts what she preached for the first ten years of her career. She has now shifted her focus to "expense management," saying that social security and Medicare may be doomed and that our 401(k) balances won't be sufficient to save us from financial catastrophe.[50] I don't want to pick on Orman for her failed predictions. Many "experts" make this mistake. However, someone like Orman who relies so much on the trust of her audience, should be more careful about "driving without a license." Even more problematic is the fact that in the last few years, Orman has given in to the temptation to leverage her popularity by entering into financial arrangements with brokers (TD Ameritrade),[51] investment managers (Mark Grimaldi),[52] and prepaid debit card issuers (the "Approved Card")[53] that seriously calls into question the independence of her advice.

All that being said, among purveyors of financial advice, I believe that Suze Orman is one of the better, or at least less harmful, ones. In fact, I believe she (at least initially) spoke to her audience out of a sincere and authentic desire to help the many people who, at the time, had nowhere else to turn. As a true pioneer in the field, she deserves some credit for opening the conversation with vast numbers of people who previously had nowhere to turn to for help. Unfortunately, many of the financial advisors who followed in her wake misled their followers and acted far more unethically than Orman. In fact, following their advice can get you into serious financial trouble.

Let's start at the top with Dave Ramsey, who, by many measures, is the most popular and influential of all of the financial planners currently providing financial advice to the general public.

Dave Ramsey and Living a Righteous Life

As I write these words, the number one bestselling author in the world of personal finance is a fanatic evangelical preacher named Dave Ramsey.[54] Ostensibly packaged as guides to financial planning, his books and sermons almost always focus on living a righteous life and being ever vigilant against the temptation of the Devil.[55] For him, the Devil is Debt. He views debt from a (literally) biblical perspective as the root of much of the evil in the world, a path to enslavement. He says that living a debt-free life should be the singular goal of any sound financial plan.

I don't doubt that Ramsey's laser-like focus on debt and the particular method he advocates for reducing/eliminating one's debts make people feel better about their financial progress. It's also possible that his approach allows some people to bring more discipline to the management of their financial life. I will even concede that, in some narrow situations, it could marginally improve a person's financial health. However, from an objective/economic perspective, it is flat out wrong in several ways and on several levels.

His debt snowball[56] plan constitutes just one example of how substantively misguided Ramsey's analysis of debt is. In his bestselling book, *The Total Money Makeover*,[57] he describes this technique for personal financial management in great detail. This method, he claims, will help you "get out of debt, give, and invest at an unbelievable rate." Essentially, what the debt snowball method says is that the way to attain financial health is to do whatever is necessary, including reducing your standard of living and/or working harder to increase your income in order to repay *all* of your debt *regardless* of what kind of debt it is *or* what the rate of interest on it is. When put like this, it sounds a little ridiculous, but I have now read this section of *Total Money Makeover*[58] several times and that is *exactly* what he is saying.

It gets worse. Not only does he say that you should work to pay off *all* your debt, but he also says that you should not start with the most expensive debt (e.g., credit card debt), but with the debt that has the lowest balance and is therefore the debt that is easiest to pay off. He goes so far as to say that in order to do that, you should reduce all your other expenses to a bare minimum *including making only minimum payments on revolving credit card debt*. He actually says that a critical part of the strategy is to "Keep paying minimums on all the debts except the smallest until it is paid."[59] This is not only very bad advice, but following it blindly can get you in real trouble. Let's take a look at just how dangerous and potentially destructive to your financial life this strategy can be.

Consider first the numerical example that Ramsey uses to demonstrate why the debt snowball is such a powerful strategy. He describes a "typical American with a $50,000 income" as paying $1,995 per month in loan repayments of various sorts, including car and mortgage payments, minimum credit card payments, a student loan, and some "miscellaneous debt." Ramsey then says that if, instead of making those monthly $1,995 payments, this family were able to invest those amounts in a mutual fund, they would have over $1 million after fifteen years and $5.5 million after twenty-eight years. This is, to put it mildly, a highly misleading assertion.

First, and perhaps most egregiously, the rate of return that Ramsey is assuming on the mutual fund investment is unrealistically high. In particular, he is assuming an annual return of slightly more than 12 percent. He seems to actually believe this is reasonable as he says at the very beginning of the book that, in general, you should invest in "good growth stock mutual funds" as they "should make 12 percent on your money over time."[60] To emphasize this point, he states explicitly that "Any decent broker with the heart of a teacher can, in his or her sleep, lead you to funds with long track records averaging over 12 percent. So, don't let anyone tell you that you can't predict a 12 percent rate when you are considering investments for ten years or longer." This statement as we have seen earlier is directly contradicted by history, current economic theory, and our growing understanding of the uncertainty and unpredictability of the future.

Beyond that, the comparison itself is flawed. For one thing, Ramsey seems to suggest that the entire $1,995 monthly payment that this family is making is being used to pay the *interest* on their debt, rather than the debt itself. In fact, a good portion of the $1,995 in monthly payments *is already being used to pay off the debt*. By my estimate, almost $900 (or 45 percent) of the $1,995 is going toward paying principal, while actual interest payments are only about $1,100 per month. The fact that mortgage interest is generally tax-deductible means that, after taxes, less than $1,000 per month of this typical consumer's income is being used to pay interest, so it is only this smaller amount that Ramsey should compare to alternative investments. In other words, if you have debt, eventually you will need to pay it off. The only savings you get from doing so faster will be in the form of interest payments that will no longer be required.

In order to demonstrate numerically how faulty the debt snowball strategy is, I deconstructed Ramsey's example and backed into the make-up of the actual debts, including developing estimates of what the likely interest rates and pay-off periods might be. There are many possibilities, but below is one reasonable scenario.

Type of debt	Amount owed	Interest rate	Monthly payment	Pay-off period
Mortgage	$130,000	6 percent	$850	25 years
Student Loan	$20,000	8 percent	$165	20 years
Credit Card	$12,000	15 percent	$185	12 years
Miscellaneous	$7,500	8 percent	$120	7 years
Car #1	$21,000	5 percent	$495	4 years
Car #2	$7,500	5 percent	$180	4 years
TOTAL	$198,000	6.7 percent	$1,995	

Even if I have gotten the specifics slightly wrong, the nature of the debts that Ramsey describes are such that my observations below should be valid regardless of the actual situation he used for his example.

The first thing to notice about the table above is that one, and only one, of the debts shown is charging a rate higher than 12 percent. If Ramsey is right that by investing in stocks one can earn a steady 12 percent return over the next thirty years, then logically it would *not* be advisable to pay off *any* of those debts *except* the credit card. You can see this by imagining how much "free money" you could earn by borrowing money at 8 percent and then investing the proceeds at 12 percent. You could pay the interest on your loan and, with your 12 percent return, still put a 4 percent profit (12 percent minus 8 percent) in your pocket. Even more importantly, it should be obvious that no matter what else is done later, the *first* thing that this typical American should do with any extra dollars that can be freed up by controlling expenses or working harder is to pay off their credit card balance. By doing so, he/she will effectively be earning a 15 percent return on his/her money. Now *that's* a good deal, and a much better bet than investing in the stock market.

With respect to the other debts, if one is going to simply "go by the numbers," the choices get a little trickier. If you are less optimistic about the stock market, you might consider early repayment of the student loan and/or the miscellaneous debt. Doing so is tantamount to getting a *guaranteed 8 percent return* on those extra payments. Depending on your view of the stock market, those debt repayments could very well be a sounder investment than taking your chances on the roller coaster ride of a mutual fund investment. To me the idea of early repayment of the car and mortgage loans is, in this particular case, probably wrong and a waste of money that could be more effectively deployed elsewhere. This is because the after-tax interest rate on these loans is so low that most people can find better investments/uses of the money (maybe even in the stock market).

My only caveat for my observations above is that how much debt to take on and maintain is a complicated and not fully quantitative question because carrying a large amount of outstanding debt (mortgage, car, or otherwise) creates leverage and some risk in your personal balance sheet.

As we have already discussed, leverage makes your financial status more fragile. We will delve more deeply into this issue again in Chapter 14.

Ramsey's view is that prioritizing repayments to pay off the smallest debts first will encourage more fiscal discipline. First, I am far from convinced that he is qualified to provide advice on what is essentially a behavioral economics question. Even more importantly, this strategy is highly inefficient and risky from a financial perspective because it effectively extends the aggregate repayment period for all debts, exposing the family to the serious risk of unforeseen financial setbacks, causing them to fall behind on one or more of the larger debts that have been put on the back burner while these smaller debts are being paid off one by one.

The notion that the state of our financial distress should be measured by the *number* of debts outstanding (or worse, by the number we have actually paid off) strikes me as ludicrous. If my reconstruction of the outstanding balances and interest rate charged on the loans to this typical American is even remotely reasonable, then the debt snowball strategy Dave recommends will likely cost this family *thousands of dollars in extra finance charges and lost investment income* beyond what they would have paid/received had they simply made the payments as scheduled, using any money they could afford to save *after* making the $1,995 per month payment to pay off their credit card debt and then invest the rest. Even greater savings could be had by adopting the more rational strategy of accelerating the repayment of *some* of the loans, starting with the ones charging the highest rate of interest and stopping when you get to ones charging interest rates *below* what could be earned by investing the money instead of repaying debt.

Perhaps by now you have heard enough about Ramsey's misguided strategy, but there is one more important point to think about and one that is highly relevant to the basic premise of this book. That is, that even if the debt snowball didn't have the deeply flawed structure that it does, there is a much more fundamental problem with his approach. Specifically, with the complexity of almost everyone's financial life, as well as the overwhelming complexity of financial markets and the system in general, such a simple solution can't possibly be the universal answer to people's problems. As Sylvia Porter said, but so many have forgotten, there is *no such thing* as a typical American family.[61] Everyone's particular situation is unique, and even if different individuals might look the same "on paper," each of us have our own values that cause us to weigh both risk and future possibilities very differently. Each of us needs to decide for ourselves where to walk in this financial wilderness, which mountains we want to climb, how much bad weather we are willing to endure, and ultimately, where we want to pitch our tent and how we want to live.

We discussed the history of money in Section I. As we saw, the invention of debt and interest was one of the early and very controversial technological enhancements to facilitate money's function as a medium of exchange. Debt and interest allowed exchanges of goods and services to take place with time lags between the provision and receipt of those goods and services. Since then, the amount, as well as the number of types and uses of debt, has exploded. As we have all seen, an enormous variety of loans have emerged in the last few hundred years, along with enhancements to the basic concept of debt. These loans include fixed and variable mortgages, credit cards, investment margins, and student loans, among others. Debt itself is now too complex to be treated so simplistically. When it is embedded in its many forms into our lives, the question of "Is debt good?" becomes meaningless. As HFW Principle #2 states, how you handle debt is absolutely critical to your financial well-being. However, decisions about debt must be made holistically and in context.

Bad and wrongheaded as Dave Ramsey's advice on debt and investment returns might be, it is actually his blatant conflicts of interest that bother me the most. As noted earlier, Suze Orman likely crossed an ethical line when she started associating herself with and making money from specific products and services (e.g., the Market Navigator newsletter) about which she was also theoretically providing independent advice. But Orman's transgressions pale in comparison to Ramsey, who takes "conflict of interest" to an entirely new level. In addition to leveraging the popularity of his radio show[62] to generate revenue from other less pure sources, e.g., advertising by insurance brokers, he actually makes money through the "Dave Ramsey-Endorsed Local Provider Program"[63] by recommending *other* financial planners who themselves are conflicted by providing investment advice that is less than independent due to their receipt of commissions on investments they recommend.

That millions of vulnerable consumers have bought Dave Ramsey's books and continue to follow his destructive advice is tragic, but in my mind, he is only the most blatant example of what is wrong with the financial planning industry. As we see in the next chapter, there are many others who are misleading the public in other subtle and not-so-subtle ways.

Chapter 5
Charlatans, Fools, and Snake Oil Salesmen

Do you believe in magic?

I don't know about you, but I love magic shows. It's not just the amazement I feel watching someone do something that seems impossible, making me wonder, "How in the world did he do that?" It's more than that. It is something primal and exciting. Watching a true master of these dark arts, I become a little kid who *wants* to believe that it really *is* magic that I'm watching and that the mysterious man on stage has tapped into forces that truly exist but no one but him can use. I know better now, of course, but when someone explains how a trick is actually done, I still can't help but be a little disappointed as the world returns to spinning in its normal, if confusing, way.

We all secretly want to believe in magic, and I think that is particularly true when it comes to financial matters where we often feel imprisoned and want desperately to be able to magically shed our shackles and escape our predicament. It's that desire that many of the purveyors of financial advice are tapping into. And just like the kid who, after watching Houdini do it, thinks he can jump into a lake with a straitjacket on and escape without drowning, we need to recognize the reality of what we are watching and not try to do it ourselves until and unless we thoroughly understand exactly how the trick is done and have developed the skills to actually "perform" the magic that we see on stage.

So, at the risk of disillusioning many of you who are looking for miraculous escapes from financial troubles, I am going to explain some of the techniques that financial wizards (particularly the ones you see on TV) use to fool you into thinking there is an easy solution to your financial issues.

Just like any good magician, financial advisors are adept at psychological manipulation. In performing any magic trick, it is essential to get the audience looking in the wrong place and/or focusing on the wrong object. When it comes to financial matters, it is relatively easy to misdirect and mislead us. Not only are we not rational financial decision-makers, being prone to strong emotional biases as well as basic fear and greed, we are also hard-wired to have cognitive biases and make systematic errors, all of which an advisor can take advantage of. When we talk about these human factors in Section IV, it will be clear *why* we are taken in by the many advisors out there who are interested in telling you how to manage your financial life. What I want to do now is talk about *how* they do it.

Among the more prevalent techniques you will come across are the "smoke and mirrors" that surround many financial strategies. The advisor will often provide a lot of seemingly important information that is actually irrelevant to your basic financial issues.

A description of the variety and extent of this kind of misdirection could fill a chapter all by itself. Rather than delve into the ways you can get lost in a thicket of distractions, I would just advise steering clear of any book that purports to "educate" on the details of phenomena that may or may not be relevant to your particular situation (e.g., how the future of AI may change the way you invest your money). Much of such writing might be well-intentioned and well-researched, but it almost certainly won't be directly relevant to financial decisions requiring your immediate attention.

One example of what I mean can be seen in Ric Edelman's best-selling *The Truth About Your Future: The Money Guide You Need Now, Later, and Much Later.*[64] Edelman is actually quite smart and a very good writer. He is also a close colleague of friends of mine. I have great respect for Edelman and his communication skills. I also have no reason to doubt his ethics or his good intentions. That being said, I believe his method of exposition can easily lead you to make important financial decisions for the wrong reasons.

Another, and potentially more harmful, form of misdirection used by financial advisors is representing *correlation* as *causation*. This is a big problem and it has plagued scientists and other truth seekers for thousands of years, so its prevalence in the financial planning world is not surprising. The difference is that where scientists are always on guard against confusing the two and go to great lengths to avoid making this mistake, financial planners seem either unaware of its existence or happily take advantage of their audience's weakness in detecting the difference.

To give one blatant example of confusing correlation with causation, consider Chapter 1 of *You Can Retire Sooner Than You Think* by Wes Moss[65] (#18 on Amazon's personal finance bestseller list). In this chapter, Moss attempts to give his readers some advice on how to be a "happy retiree." To do this, he first does "research." As Moss says, "In my comprehensive survey of 1,350 retirees across 46 states I was ruthless in my quest for answers."[66] He even "went to the Georgia Tech Department of Mathematics and had the data's 'confidence and significance' verified by the former president of the GA Tech Math Club, along with one of her former math professors."[67] And what did he come up with? Well, it seems that among his "significant" findings was that happy retirees "don't drive BMWs, but unhappy retirees often do." On the basis of this "research," Moss then advises you to "Ditch the BMW and stick to Asian brands."[68] Hopefully it is clear that Moss is mistaking correlation for causation. It may be that unhappy retirees own BMWs, but that is *much* different from saying that buying a BMW will *cause* you to become an unhappy retiree.

While buying the right car is not going to make the difference between a happy and an unhappy retirement, one other conclusion Moss draws from his survey that also confuses correlation and causation goes right to the heart of how to manage what is, for most people, their biggest financial asset. Specifically, he finds that happy retirees "didn't have a mortgage (and) if they did, their payoff was in sight."[69] He then concludes that to be happy in retirement, one should strive to own one's home free and clear. Moss incorporates this "insight" into his recommended financial strategy. He even calls it Secret #3 in his "5 Money Secrets of Happy Retirees."[70] Describing this part of his "5 Secrets"-based financial strategy, he says that you should do whatever's necessary to "pay off your mortgage in as little as five years."[71] Again, it may very well be that having no mortgage *correlates* with being a happy retiree, but that doesn't mean that paying yours off will make you one. How to handle this significant asset, and the typically very large liability (i.e., the mortgage) that goes along with it, is a very complicated question and one that simply can't be answered outside of the context of your entire financial situation. We will talk much more about this in Section V, but for now, it's important that you realize that the strategy that Moss outlines (including Secret #3) is based on a flawed premise. You need to be aware of this dangerous and misleading trap that can get you to mistake the *manifestation* of good financial decisions for the *method* of making good choices.

There are plenty of other psychological tricks that advisors utilize in misleading you. We will spend much of Section IV discussing the emotional biases we have and the cognitive "bugs" that make us vulnerable to such tactics. Now, however, it's time to get a bit technical and talk about some of the specific "money technologies" that will allow you to understand the "magic" that is part of the performance of many of the financial "gurus" you read, listen to, or watch.

Inside the Black Bag of Tricks—Interest, Leverage, and "Backfitting a 'Winning' Strategy"

Almost since the concept of money earning interest was invented over a thousand years ago, people became aware of its remarkable ability to turn modest sums of money into fortunes. Albert Einstein called compound interest the "eighth wonder of the world" and said famously that "he who understands it earns it...he who doesn't, pays it."[72] Mathematically, the concept is very simple. If I can earn 10 percent annually on my money and invest $1,000, after one year I will have $1,100, but after two years I will have not just $1,200, but $1,210. This extra $10 comes from the fact that there is *interest earned on the interest itself.* While this difference is initially small, over time it becomes very significant. If I earn 10 percent interest for ten years, rather than have $2,000 ($1,000 plus ten times the one hundred dollars of interest I earned in the first year) I will have about $2,600. The emergence of this extra "interest on the interest" often seems like magic, and in the hands of an unscrupulous advisor, it can be used to devastating effect.

Consider Ramsey's example discussed earlier. He described how, by simply setting aside a modest $1,995 per month it was possible to accumulate $1 million in only fifteen years and $5.5 million in less than thirty years.[73] How did he do it? Well, he took the concept of compound interest and used three of its inherent properties to make his demonstration even more dramatic than it otherwise would have been. First, rather than tell you that you were actually investing over $350,000 (fifteen years of monthly payments of $1,995) to accumulate your first million, he broke the investment into very small periodic payments. Using periodic payments with compounding interest will often make for much more dramatic comparisons as our minds tend to focus on the huge difference between the $1,995 and the $1 million, rather than thinking about the fact that, in this case, you will have to make *180 separate payments of $1,995* to get there.

There are two other "dials" Ramsey used to make his example so striking. First, he used an interest rate of about 12 percent instead of a more "normal" investment return on stocks of say 7 or 8 percent (I put quotes around the word *normal* because I actually don't believe there is such a thing as normal when it comes to returns on something as complex and volatile as the stock market). But the important point is that if Ramsey had used 8 percent instead of 12 percent, your $350,000 of payments would have only turned into a little more than $750,000. This is still a nice return, but not as "magical" as what Ramsey is saying.

It goes without saying that the higher the interest rate, the more spectacular the accumulation of money looks. But what many people fail to realize is how sensitive to small changes in interest rates that accumulation is. It is important, then, that whenever you see an illustration of some investment compounding over a long period of time, you scrutinize the assumed interest rate *very* carefully. This brings me to the final aspect of Ramsey's example—the time period over which the accumulation occurs. In the investment world, fifteen years is a *very long time,* and to assume that you will get *any* consistent rate of return (particularly when you are talking about a volatile investment like stocks) over that period is, in my view, very risky. And just like the interest rate, the amount of money that you end up with is highly sensitive to the period over which you are investing. In Ramsey's example, even using a 12 percent return, after ten years (vs. fifteen years) you would have only $440,000 and not the $1 million he promised.

There is perhaps no better example of how compound interest can mislead than the famous "Give up your daily Starbucks latte and retire early" advice first put forth by David Bach.[74] Bach suggests that by giving up your daily latte, you can save three dollars per day. This translates to twenty dollars per week and $1,000 per year. Bach suggests (just like Ramsey) that you can then invest this $1,000 per year in the stock market and, after a few decades, have a significant supplement to your retirement savings. He even calls it "the Latte Factor" in the retirement strategy he recommends. In a sense, he has taken this magic trick to its logical extreme, breaking the investment into even smaller pieces than Dave Ramsey and having it accumulate over an even longer period of time.

If compound interest was the only trick that financial advisors had, it would be a relatively straightforward task to deconstruct and understand the advice of your financial advisor. Unfortunately, there are two other more sophisticated techniques that advisors use to seduce you into using financial strategies that are either far riskier than they appear or simply won't work. The most dangerous of these techniques are those that rely on "leverage"—a term we introduced at the beginning of this book.

We have already noted how taking on debt adds leverage to your financial situation and makes it fragile. Now it is time to dig a little deeper into how financial advisors use it to mislead you. In the hands of an unscrupulous advisor, the idea of leverage can create some dazzling visions of potential riches for gullible consumers. In its purest form, leverage simply means borrowing at a low interest rate and investing the proceeds at a higher rate. So, for example, there are many investment brokers who will be happy to set up a "margin" account for you that will allow you to borrow money at a relatively low rate (as I write this, Fidelity Investments is advertising "margin rates as low as 4.25 percent") and then invest it in something (e.g., stock mutual funds) that will earn a higher rate (e.g., 7 or 8 percent). Typically, the only restriction that a broker places on this loan is that the loan can never be more than actual funds you have on deposit (e.g., if you have $5,000 invested, you can borrow any amount up to another $5,000). The reason it is called leverage is because, in order to get this opportunity, you need to invest a certain amount of money, which is then leveraged by borrowing against it to turn it into more money than would be possible by simply investing your original sum.

This is analogous to using a mechanical lever to lift a weight that you could not lift with your hands. For example, let's say you open up an investment account at Schwab with $1,000. If you were to invest that sum in a stock mutual fund, you could perhaps expect to earn 8 percent per year over the long term. After ten years, you would have about $2,150. However, let's say that instead of doing that, you decided to leverage that initial investment by borrowing another $1,000 "on margin." Let's assume that Schwab will charge you 5 percent for that money and you don't have to pay it or the interest back until you close your account. Now, you can invest $2,000 into that mutual fund (your original $1,000 plus the $1,000 you borrowed). After ten years, your account will grow to $4,300, but you will only owe Schwab $1,600 (your $1,000 loan plus ten years of interest at 5 percent per year). Let's say you now decide to pay back the loan and close your account. You will walk away with $2,700 instead of the $2,150 you would have had if you just invested the $1,000 without leveraging it. By this "magic" trick, you have converted a pretty ordinary 8 percent return into a much more spectacular 10.4 percent annual return.

Is there a catch? You bet. First of all, for leverage to work, you must be absolutely sure you can invest the money you borrow in a way that will earn you more than the interest rate you are being charged on the loan. That, in and of itself, is no easy task as banks and other lenders are trying to make a profit. If *they* could earn a higher rate on their money than they could by lending it to you, they may very well might. But let's say they are not in a position to do so (e.g., Schwab might not be allowed to invest their own corporate funds in stocks that they also broker). Even so, you might not earn the expected 8 percent return *every year*, and in those years where your investment doesn't perform as expected, you will be left owing a greater percentage of your investment account than you anticipated. This is the fragility we discussed earlier. It is dangerous for two reasons; first, because it exposes you to further drops in value that could *wipe out your entire investment*, and second, even if it doesn't wipe you out, it can disrupt your investment strategy. For example, in this case, it could subject you to a "margin call," where Schwab will insist that you sell your stocks in order to pay back the loan. This will come at *exactly* the wrong time, that is, after there has been a drop in the stock market and before it has had time to recover.

This basic trick has many variations. There are many investment strategies where leverage is hard to observe and its operation (and risks) can get very complicated to figure out. For many years during my career as an actuary, I consulted with companies who had entered into "collateral assignment split dollar insurance programs" where leverage was the key to "supercharging" the investment returns on normal life insurance policies to fund executive retirement benefits. These deals were so complicated and the risks so well-hidden that even some of the most sophisticated financial executives in the US were surprised when the programs "crashed and burned," leaving both the executives and the company with losses that they never anticipated. My point is that anyone can get fooled by leverage, and you need to be *very* suspicious when you hear about an investment strategy that you don't fully understand and appears to generate returns much greater than you can get otherwise.

This is not to say that leverage is always a bad thing. Quite the contrary, it can be a very good thing indeed. There is one area of most people's financial lives where leverage is often appropriately present. But this is also the area where some of the most egregious and misleading strategies have been proposed by financial planners. That is in the area of real estate.

In the introduction to this book, I described how I used leverage to begin accumulating real estate, which today contributes materially to my financial security. I am not alone in using leverage; many people have become wealthy in the same way. Countless books, workshops, and TV shows, among others, have been produced before *and* after the real estate collapse of 2008–2009, promoting the idea that to become wealthy, all you need to do is borrow money to invest in real estate (rental, commercial, or residential). By now, almost everyone has heard (and hopefully rejected) those get-rich-quick schemes associated with buying real estate with "no money down" (essentially being indefinitely leveraged), and then flipping the house for "free money." Nevertheless, I would be remiss if I didn't highlight this attractive but dangerous trail that leads up to some high peaks, but whose footing can be extremely treacherous.

That doesn't mean you shouldn't consider this route to financial security. If you do take this trail, do remember that house prices can go down as well as up. If you know what you are getting into, accepting leverage can mean that buying a house (even a second home) could be one of the best (but not risk-free) investments you can ever make. In the final section of this book, when we discuss the tools to put in your backpack, we will also dig deeper into how to prudently use this trick.

"Backfitting," however, is an entirely different matter. In my view, this is one of the most abused and little understood sleights of hand that financial advisors use to give consumers misguided confidence in their investment strategy. It has been developed by looking at investments that have been successful in the past and naively assuming that the same strategy will be successful in the future. There are (literally) almost an infinite variety of ways to do this, and that is exactly the point. A great many failed predictions arise from economists and others developing models that reproduce the past but have nothing meaningful to say about the future. Similarly, it is pretty easy to comb through the historical data and find a (sometimes very complicated) investment strategy that *would have* produced spectacular returns in the past, but that is not the same as developing a strategy that will generate good returns in the future.

The simplest and most common version of a backfitted strategy was described earlier by Dave Ramsey when he put forth the proposition that any "decent broker with the heart of a teacher" could find you "funds with long track records averaging over 12 percent," and therefore, by investing in those funds, you can assume you will earn 12 percent *in the future*. This statement illustrates the two fundamental problems with backfitted strategies. First and most importantly, as noted above, the past is *no guarantee whatsoever* for what will happen in the future. Beyond that, there is significant survival bias at play when you look at the track records of specific investment managers or funds. In Chapter 11, we will talk about survival bias again, but for now just note that even if *all* the stock funds you looked at had a decent historical return, you are still being overly optimistic, because you are not considering the funds that had such a poor return that they did not survive to the present.

I remember watching one of the clearest demonstrations of survival bias many years ago when I attended a large lecture on the subject. There were several hundred of us in the audience, and the lecturer asked all of us to stand up, take a coin out of our pocket and flip it. Those who got heads were asked to remain standing while those who got tails were asked to sit down. Then he repeated the process several more times. After seven flips, there was one man still standing who had gotten seven heads in a row. The lecturer then addressed him and asked "What's your secret?"

I hope the example above is enough to convince you that there is no magic to those funds that your advisor tells you are special because of their stellar track records. As noted earlier, backfitted strategies can get much more sophisticated than simply finding a manager who has been lucky enough to have "outperformed" his/her competitors. The strategies themselves can be extremely complex and are often presented in a way that is designed to make you feel that there is a great deal of science behind the method. In fact, many of the "algorithms" that certain hedge funds use have been developed in this way. These are funds that institutions often invest millions of dollars in, hoping to receive the same kind of returns in the future that the algorithm has generated in the past.

There are other tricks of the trade that advisors use to fool you, but the ones described here are the basics and should give you the confidence and skepticism to be entertained, but not fooled, by the magic show that the personal finance advisor industry is currently performing. So far, by design, I have focused on the more popular and mass market personal finance advisors, because I believe that, for the most part, you should avoid listening to them.

This doesn't mean that I think you can do it all by yourself. In fact, almost everyone will need help at some point. Figuring out when to seek help, and where to go to find what you need, is the subject we will now address.

Chapter 6
Hidden Agendas and Finding a Trustworthy Trail Guide

Use Your Money to Find Good Help

In 2008, my company transferred me to its Paris office for an assignment that would last for a year. Before I left, I had to figure out how to reorganize my financial situation so I could live there temporarily while keeping the rest of my American life (e.g., house, investments, etc.) running so that it would be intact when I came back. It was a complicated problem as I needed the ability to transfer money back and forth between the two countries to have euros to spend in France while also managing my US investments and continuing to pay ongoing bills (e.g., insurance, utilities on my home) to companies in the US.

I discovered pretty quickly that I needed a global bank to meet my needs, and after investigating a few, I decided that HSBC[75] was the one best suited for my particular situation. The key was that HSBC had a Paris branch located just a few blocks from my new office, and they had an easy-to-use online banking portal that would allow me to transfer money freely between my US and French checking accounts. I also discovered that HSBC could handle the rest of my US banking needs while I was overseas, and that if I moved my retirement account there (I had a rollover IRA with about $500,000 from a previous employer), I would qualify for premier status and get access to many benefits that regular customers of the bank did not enjoy.

This was an added bonus I was not expecting, and I was happily surprised when I discovered that Tyson, the investment advisor I chose among the several alternatives that HSBC offered me, was a guy who was not going to try and sell me anything *and* was *not* going to receive any commissions on trades he performed on my behalf. In fact, Tyson was paid a base salary and a bonus (based in part on my happiness and in part on the size of the assets his clients kept at the bank). This meant that his incentives, while perhaps not perfectly aligned with my investment objectives, were at least not in direct conflict with them.

It was even better than that. In addition to being able to use Tyson's expertise, by being a premier customer, I had access to many other financial professionals who were there to assist me. There was a banker who could help me organize my bill paying, there were insurance specialists who could help me find coverages I might need on my cars and other property, and best of all, they introduced me to Natasha Burton, a loan officer who could help me with any mortgage or real estate financing I might need.

Like the other service providers offered to me, Natasha was paid on a base and bonus basis, and therefore was able to give me unbiased advice unaffected by any commission she might make on my mortgage. As a result, she was entirely different from the many mortgage brokers I had used to buy and refinance the many houses I had owned since I bought that first townhouse in 1980.

Natasha not only had a razor-sharp mind, but her knowledge of the mortgage business as well as the wide array of loans that HSBC offered was encyclopedic. She also very quickly understood that as an actuary, I was not her usual customer. She became more of a collaborator than a service provider. Together, we analyzed in detail the fixed, variable, long- and short-term mortgage loans that the bank had to offer, choosing the one whose combination of rate, duration, and features provided the most value. Because I was a premier customer, HSBC was willing to give me a mortgage loan using a lower interest rate than that available to other customers. HSBC also offered its premier customers special kinds of loans (e.g., a mortgage under which I paid interest only at a guaranteed rate for five years) that were not generally available in the marketplace.

The fact that Natasha's compensation was not affected by which loan I chose meant that I could be confident that she was working completely for me and had no hidden agenda as so many loan brokers do.

In the decade that I've known her, Natasha has refinanced my Berkeley house twice and helped me get three more mortgage loans on other real estate I've purchased since, each time saving me thousands of dollars versus what those loans would have cost me had I not kept my money at HSBC. Natasha has become an integral member of the team of experts I use to maintain my financial health, and I have become a loyal customer of HSBC.

Why HSBC hired someone like Natasha stems from the business model that many (but not all) big banks adopt. These institutions use a relationship model rather than a transactional one. Specifically, what HSBC, along with other global multiline financial institutions, discovered is that by focusing on their biggest customers and providing those customers with access to their best people, the bank will be able to bring in and retain more assets (a source of profitability as we saw in Chapter 2). As a result, they will be able to provide other profitable services to those customers without having to utilize commission-based salespeople who not only don't always have their clients' best interests in mind, but also tend to job hop, creating disruption in service and causing customer turnover as well. Both of these factors hurt a bank's bottom line.

Once I discovered the benefits of being a premier banking customer, I began to take advantage of this trend to find other professionals who would be 100 percent on my side as I made my way through the financial wilderness. It turns out that you don't have to deposit too much money at a given bank to qualify as a premier customer. At some banks, it takes no more than $100,000. That may seem like a lot of money, but most of us will have that much in at least one of our 401(k) or IRA accounts. By spreading your money around to different banks who use the relationship model, you can have access to each institution's stable of highly qualified professionals who, while not necessarily as competent as Natasha, will at least have their compensation incentives structured in a way that lets you trust that they are looking out for you. I eventually spread my retirement accounts around and became a premier customer at three other banks—US Bancorp, Chase, and Wells Fargo. Not only do I now get access to a variety of financial experts when I run up against specific needs, but when the next financial crisis occurs and banks become stressed, having money in several institutions should provide me some protection against any one of those banks failing.

This technique has served me well, and while Natasha has since left HSBC for other ventures, Tyson (now at US Bancorp) continues to advise me on my investments. My relationships at each of my four banks continue to allow me access to all the help I need.

Unfortunately, just putting your money into a big bank and relying on their experts is not enough to maintain your financial wellness. You also need to be able to figure out *what* kind of help you need and *when* you need it. For this, you need to educate yourself and find information you can trust. As we have seen before, many, if not most, of the books that are published purporting to educate you have been written by financial experts who themselves have a hidden agenda and do not have your best interests in mind. The good news is that there are some brilliant minds out there who do publish insights and analysis that you can find to help you understand key aspects of the financial challenges that you may be facing now or will face in the future.

They are not easy to find, but they are out there and well worth looking for.

Find and Follow Truth Seekers

The first time I met Barry Sacks was over twenty years ago. One of my clients hired him to solve a fiendishly complex tax/legal problem that had arisen in the bargaining between my client and its major union. Arriving a few minutes late, he was clearly excited, but not about the tax issue. After some brief hellos, he told us about the brilliant idea he had for a new invention that had occurred to him on his way over to the meeting. Pulling a single credit card from his overstuffed wallet, he asked us to consider all the wasted space ("real estate" as he put it) on the card that currently was taken up by a bank logo and a background picture. Specifically, he asked, why couldn't all that space be used to incorporate the information that all of the other cards in his wallet contained? Just like the universal remotes that were then all the rage in the electronics industry, he suggested that with his innovation, we all could have a "Unicard" that could be used for all the electronic transactions that we currently conduct, from department store purchases to borrowing books from the local library. As Barry waxed eloquent about all the convenience and financial efficiencies of such an invention, as well as the easily surmountable technical challenges associated with its introduction, the client and I sat there both enthralled and a little taken aback at the unexpected turn the meeting had taken.

As I got to know Barry better, I found that this incident was by no means an unusual occurrence with this curious and creative polymath. With a Ph.D. in physics from MIT, Barry had started his career in academia and was well on his way to becoming a tenured professor when he decided that tax law would be much more interesting than electromagnetism and lecturing undergraduate students. He went back to law school and very quickly became one of the leading ERISA[76] attorneys in the Bay area. By the time we met, he was a partner at one of San Francisco's boutique law firms and a specialist in the complex and unusual legal issues that often arise in the pension world. Many of these problems had actuarial aspects and, as a result, Barry and I got to collaborate on a number of fascinating client projects over the years.

Despite his demanding day job, Barry is an unapologetic out-of-the-box thinker who constantly comes up with new ideas and new approaches to old problems. He currently holds several patents (not including his idea for the "Unicard," which, in some ways, has been incorporated into smartphone technology) in fields ranging from physics to financial engineering. His current passion is reverse mortgages and how this obscure, much-maligned, and poorly understood financial vehicle can be used in creative ways to not only augment one's retirement income, but also to become an integral part of a "decumulation" strategy after retirement. Barry's 2012 groundbreaking article in the *Journal of Financial Planning* ("Reversing the Conventional Wisdom: Using Home Equity to Supplement Retirement Income")[77] showed the rest of the world how this could be done. It almost instantly rehabilitated the somewhat sordid reputation that reverse mortgages had historically suffered from.

A Reverse Mortgage Credit Line is actually nothing more than a loan against the value of your home. It operates just like a traditional home equity line of credit (HELOC), but with three crucial distinctions. First, unlike a HELOC, when you set up a Reverse Mortgage Credit Line, the amount you can draw down is not fixed; rather, it grows every year, and not because of any increase in the value of your house, but at a stated annual rate. So, for example, if you set up a Reverse Mortgage Credit Line for $200,000 at age sixty-five and don't use it until age seventy-five, by the time you start taking cash, the amount available might be $300,000 or even more. This, in itself, is a valuable way to assure yourself that you will have access to funds later in your retirement should you find your other sources of retirement income drying up. However, the next two differences between a HELOC and a reverse mortgage credit line are even more important. The second difference is *you don't have to pay any interest or principal on the reverse mortgage until you sell or move out of your house,* and the final difference is that, unlike a traditional mortgage, when you take out a reverse mortgage, *you will never have to pay back more than the actual value of your home regardless of the amount of debt you accumulate on the house.*

These last two differences are what turns a reverse mortgage credit line from a source of emergency funds into a powerful retirement income generation tool that, when part of a sophisticated and highly effective decumulation strategy, can take you from a situation of having to worry about outliving your assets to one where you can comfortably draw down 6 percent, 7 percent, or even 8 percent of your savings every year and still be confident that you have very little chance of running out of money before you die.

The reason Barry's work is so important is that, in addition to highlighting how millions of future retirees can effectively utilize their biggest asset (their home) for generating retirement income, it also illustrates how important it is for *everyone* to protect themselves against "sequence of returns risk," a subtle and important danger that many of the most knowledgeable financial planners don't talk about with their clients. Sequence of returns risk refers to the fact that even if the *average* return on your investments during your retirement is good, if negative investment returns occur in the *early* years of retirement, and your retirement savings are drawn on during those the years of negative returns, the likelihood of the account becoming exhausted in the later years of retirement is much greater than if the account is *not* drawn on immediately following the negative returns. Sequence of returns risk stems directly from the volatility that is inherent in almost all investment markets. Barry's coordinated strategy minimizes the potential impact of this risk on the stability and long-term security of the retirement income many people will need to live on for the rest of their lives.

In the final section of this book, we will talk more about reverse mortgages and other underutilized tools that you may want to keep in your financial wilderness survival kit, but for now, I just want to note that the work that Barry and other honest and *independent* researchers are doing is what you need to rely on if you want to maintain your financial health over the long term. Beyond the work Barry is doing on reverse mortgages, other independent bodies doing important work in financial wellness research include the Society of Actuaries, The Stanford Center on Longevity, the Center for Retirement Research at Boston College, and the actuarial and financial planning departments at other major universities. This is not to say that other important research is not taking place at organizations with specific economic agendas (e.g., major employee benefit consulting firms, investment houses, and accounting firms), but because that research is funded by those who might profit from specific results, the conclusions and recommendations of such research must be *very* carefully reviewed.

Since no one can be expected to stay current on all this research, let alone sort through the hidden agendas that may bias some of the findings, the question arises: Where should you go for help and how can you know you can trust what you are getting? There is no simple answer to this question, but there are steps you can take.

Diving for Pearls in the Deep Blue Ocean

Shortly after reading Barry's research, I began collaborating with him on a follow-up paper incorporating a few of my own ideas on the subject of retirement income planning. As a result of that work, I was invited to join the Academy of Home Equity in Financial Planning, a group of independent researchers and financial planners within the University of Illinois Financial Planning Department whose mission is to highlight the use of home equity as a critical component of general financial planning. As with the other organizations noted above, the Academy has no agenda other than the pursuit of knowledge in this area. One thing that makes it a little different than the others mentioned is that it includes highly respected independent financial planners who don't engage in research themselves, but rather focus on how the research generated by the group can be effectively integrated into the financial advice that planners provide to their clients. One of the most impressive of this group is Marguerita (Rita) Cheng, founder and CEO of Blue Ocean Global Wealth.[78]

Modest and soft-spoken, Rita does not present herself as a typical financial advisor. Unlike many others who came late to the industry, Rita seemed destined to become a financial planner from the time she was a little girl. With two younger sisters and a father who started life in the US with seventeen dollars in his pocket, Rita grew up precocious and pragmatic. As a third grader, while other kids read comic books and fairy tales, Rita learned how to use a scientific/financial calculator and convert one currency to another. As a child, she was introduced to the world of money by her father who emigrated from China with no money but a college degree in Economics and a desire to build a better life in a new country. After supplementing his education with a graduate degree in Mathematics, Rita's father landed a job at IBM where he had a long and successful career. Beginning when she was ten years old, Rita engaged her father in long conversations about money—what it could and couldn't do, how to get it, how to manage it, and most importantly, how it worked.

Very early on, Rita internalized important insights about money that continue to inform the way she advises her clients today. Two of her favorites are "Don't spend money in the dark" and "Money can buy opportunities and peace of mind, but never measure your self-worth by your net worth." She also learned important lessons in financial planning by watching the mistakes others in her family made (e.g., Rita's father paid for the funeral of his sister-in-law who died with no money or life insurance to pay for her burial).

After graduating from the University of Maryland and spending four years working for an investment company in Japan, Rita left the brokerage world and returned to the US where she spent the next few years picking up a BS in Finance, working part-time, starting a family, and "reading every book on financial planning I could find." Then, at age thirty-two, finally feeling ready to resume her chosen career, she joined American Express as a financial planner. Despite the unspoken expectations of her bosses, Rita refused to call on her friends and family, but rather went through the brutal process of building a client base by cold-calling strangers. Because of her integrity, her persistence, and the fact that she *really* knew what she was talking about, Rita was able, over the next fourteen years, to develop a large set of clients who valued her advice and made her a highly successful adviser at one of the top national firms in the business. Her philosophical approach was always "planning first, portfolio second" and she strove to help her clients holistically—to inspire and empower them rather than to simply help them with their financial transactions.

Even though she was successful and her clients were happy, Rita was troubled by the fact that her compensation was dependent on the financial decisions her clients made (i.e., whether to buy stocks or bonds) rather than the quality of the advice or the value she delivered to the client. In 2013, she decided to form Blue Ocean Global Wealth, a firm based on the core values of integrity, authenticity, and excellence. At Blue Ocean, Rita and her colleagues provide all the financial planning and advising services that traditional planners provide, but they do so by using a completely transparent fee structure that enables the client to know that the advisor is 100 percent on their side—exactly what HFW Principle #3 suggests.

The problem is that firms like Blue Ocean are hard to find, and even when you find an advisor that appears to have the same orientation and business model as Rita, you still need to figure out whether you believe them and whether they really do have the expertise in the area you need help with. It's this latter point that brought Rita and me together in the first place.

Among her many responsibilities, Rita is highly involved with the industry's professional organization—the Financial Planning Association (FPA). She has served on the FPA Board at both the national and local level. Through her board work on industry-wide issues and her own voracious reading of financial literature, Rita got interested early on in reverse mortgages; in particular, how they might play a role in an individual's retirement income planning.

Like almost every other financial planner at the time, Rita didn't know much about the product, but unlike the majority of planners, she wanted to know more. She introduced herself to Shelley Giordano[79] and Wade Pfau[80] who, along with Barry, are two true pioneers in the field. Rita talked to experts, read the research, and made it a point to educate herself as much as she could about the subject. The reason most planners don't bother with reverse mortgages is because they can't "sell" them and make a commission. From their perspective, they would not only be providing their clients free advice, but they might in fact be *reducing* their income because any client who might use a reverse mortgage might not buy an annuity which would generate a commission for the advisor. Rita didn't have to worry about that aspect, because she charges her clients an hourly rate for planning, and the fact that she can talk about reverse mortgages in that context just makes her time more valuable.

While not an expert in reverse mortgages, Rita knows enough to clarify for her clients whether this is something they should consider. When she finds a client who might benefit from one, she directs them to someone (e.g., Barry) who is an expert and can help the client (again on a fee basis) to actually find and implement one. The same is true for other areas as well.

Take student loans, for example. We discussed in Section I how critical the decisions you make around debt are to your long-term financial health. Outside of home mortgages, student loans represent the most significant type of debt that Americans have, with almost $1.5 trillion outstanding. This amount is significantly higher than the credit card debt that Suze Orman so often talks about. Unlike credit cards which are used for an almost infinite variety of goods and services, student loans are taken out for one purpose only—to buy an education. What kind of education to get and how much value you get out of it is a highly individual matter. It is also very complicated to determine its impact on your long-term financial health since you have to offset the value of that education by a number of hard-to-quantify factors. These factors include the cost of foregone earnings (while you attend school rather than work), the upfront dollars you might pay to obtain the student loan, and the long-term cost of the student loan itself. These are just the quantifiable factors that don't consider the subjective impacts (both positive and negative) of the decision to invest in education.

When I asked Rita what she says when her clients ask how much they should be saving for college or how much in student loans they should be taking on (for themselves or their children) she said that the first thing she tells them is that they are asking the wrong question. They should be asking, "How am I going to pay for my (or my child's) education?" That will naturally lead to other questions like "How much education are you buying (e.g., college or college plus grad school)?" and "What are you getting the education for?" Eventually, Rita helps the client determine exactly what they want to get, why they are getting it, and how much it will cost.

From that point, Rita will help the client view paying for the *specific* education they want as a problem to be solved; one of the solutions could be student loans, while another could be a structured savings and investment plan. Once the client understands that, Rita can then refer the client to an expert who can find the right student loan for the client's unique situation and/or work further with the client herself to develop a savings/investment program that may or may not include a 529 account (about which Rita *is* an expert). In some cases, the client may be sufficiently capable (or learn enough from Rita) to develop a plan of their own, and that is perfectly fine with her.

While I consider the world of money to be a financial wilderness where one can get easily lost, Rita uses a different metaphor. She considers herself a "financial lifeguard"—she is there to let you know where the rip tides will pull you out to sea and what part of the beach is dangerous because sharks infest the waters. She is also there if you stray too far from shore and need help getting back to land.

It's too bad there aren't more financial planners like her.

As we saw in the first section of this book, the world of money is incredibly complex. Part of that complexity is that no one can be an expert in all areas where you may have to make important decisions. You will occasionally find someone like Rita who is generally familiar with virtually every type of financial issue that you may find, but even Rita is not an expert in all the issues that may arise. And you will often need an expert. What do you do?

I wish there were an easy answer. One possibility is to play it safe. If, for example, you find yourself in an unfamiliar wilderness where you don't know the terrain, the weather, or the natural (and unnatural) hazards that are lurking, the first thing you might do is look for a safe clear flat area, preferably near water, and just stay put for a while. By the same token, you might organize your financial life in such a way that it is simple and fully comprehensible. That way you can manage most of it yourself and only look for help when something unexpected happens, either to your money or to you.

Unfortunately, unexpected things do happen, and life, particularly financial life, tends to get complicated even when we try to keep things simple. I know mine does. You will also likely find that to get what you want, you will have to take chances and/or get involved with new kinds of financial entanglements (like student debt or a job with a complicated retirement plan). Essentially, what you want to do in life will require you to leave that safe calm spot you found by the lake and venture out into the woods or climb up to the ridge overlooking the valley you want to get to. That's when you'll need help.

I see the process in three steps. The first is to *clarify your issues*. I believe everyone can do this themselves. In fact, I don't think it is possible for anyone to do this for you. Only you know what you are trying to achieve, what is getting in the way, and what you are afraid of. Perhaps you need to educate yourself to add some specificity to your goals or enable you to formulate your questions, and maybe you need resources like this book or a life coach to think through your situation. This is fundamentally an internal step and doesn't have much to do with financial planning.

However, once you know what you fear, desire, or need to deal with, then you need to *talk to someone who knows the world of money*. Maybe you can get some free information/education from the place where you keep your money. As we discussed earlier, with enough money on deposit, the bank will be only too happy to provide you with basic information on the transactions you want to consider. Note that if you do ask your bank, unless you are a premier customer of a relationship model bank, you need to be attentive to all the cautions and the hidden agendas that we talked about in the last chapter.

If you are willing to pay, maybe hire someone like Rita for a few hours to help you figure out the path(s) that you need to follow and the financial transactions you should be considering. A good planner should then be able to identify experts you can trust who can implement the actions you decide on as well as the cost, benefits, and risks associated with the route you want to follow. You may also do both; get two or more opinions on your situation. After all, every financial planner will have their own perspective and areas of the financial world where they are more or less comfortable. They will also have specific biases and preferences. If they are honest and good (and if you are paying them) they should be willing to share the limits of their expertise and their subjective opinions about financial matters with you.

Finally, once you have done your internal work, integrated with any assessment of your situation that a knowledgeable advisor provides, only then should you work toward implementing your plan. Investing, taking on debt, buying insurance, or even switching careers are all, in concept, like buying any kind of consumer product. You want to make sure that what you are getting is exactly what you want. You don't want to rush, and you should make sure, perhaps by comparison shopping, that you are getting a quality product at the lowest possible price.

Managing your financial health is also similar in many respects to managing your physical health. What it takes to stay alive and healthy financially requires just the same self-empowerment, research, and due diligence as what it takes to live long and stay healthy physically. Choosing and consulting with a doctor, whether a generalist or a specialist, is just one part of the process. Taking responsibility for your own well-being is also paramount, and choosing to implement a regimen or medical procedure is a decision not to be undertaken lightly. It should be done with a full understanding of the costs, benefits, and potential consequences entailed in your choice. The same is true with your money.

Unfortunately, staying alive and healthy also takes some luck. That is what we will talk about next. As vigilant and clear as we are in planning and making financial choices, the future is uncertain, far more uncertain and unpredictable than most people think. In the next few chapters, we will explore this strange territory that we call the future and discover that, while we cannot ever know what *will* happen, we can determine what *might* happen and even, to a certain degree, understand the workings of the mysterious engine that turns today into tomorrow.

SECTION III

Thinking About the Future—It's an Uncertain World

Chapter 7
The Geography of Uncertainty and "What Comes Next?"

"What quality form(s) a Man of Achievement (is) Negative Capability, that is, when a man is capable of being in uncertainties, mysteries, doubts, without any irritable reaching after fact and reason."—John Keats 1817[81]

Most of us can't handle uncertainty. Maybe we can handle it, but we certainly don't like it, and we do everything we can to eliminate it from our lives. Worse, when we can't eliminate it, we deny it, fear it, or call it risk and then try to manage it. We suffer because of uncertainty. For many people, the uncertainty surrounding money and their financial future can be crippling. I am not here to provide a way to get rid of the "expanding funnel of doubt" that is the future, but I do think I can shed some light on the nature of that unknown territory and help you survey the wild and treacherous landscape that lies between where we are now and where we are headed.

I expect that getting a better understanding of the nature of uncertainty may scare you, but I think it may also disabuse you of the notion that others know more than you about what is coming. You may get a better view of the dangers that lie ahead. You may even achieve Keats's "negative capability," which, I believe, will go a long way toward helping you survive (financially and otherwise) with the unavoidable burden of not knowing what the future holds.

The Future as a "What Comes Next?" Problem

When I was in second grade, my mathematician father gave me a book of number puzzles, both to keep me out of trouble and to introduce me to the world in which he lived. While I didn't follow his path up to the highest peaks of mathematical abstractions, I did love that book and, in particular, the many "What comes next?" problems that it contained. I got very good at solving such problems, and in a very real sense, that is what I have spent most of my adult life doing—trying to figure out what comes next and how what has happened before can give us clues as to what will happen in the future. I would go even further and say that one way to think about uncertainty itself is to consider it as one giant "What comes next?" problem. The trick, however, is that before you can even attempt to solve such a problem, you need to know what *kind* of problem you are dealing with.

In my puzzle book, each problem had an answer that you could look up in the back, but it is not so simple in real life. As I got older, I began to appreciate that there are actually two different kinds of uncertainty; one with definitive answers based on a deterministic process and one produced by a random or stochastic process. Even within these two types of processes, there are important variations, each one requiring different tools and attitudes to navigate.

To explore this terrain more closely, I want to look at some different kinds of "What comes next?" problems drawn from both where the future is theoretically knowable and from where randomness rules. We will see that there is a vast difference in how solvable those different kinds of problems are. It is even more daunting to know that when we are faced with the need to predict, we will very often not be able to tell what part of that wilderness we find ourselves in.

Traveling in the Land of Determinism

Think about the following "What comes next?" problem: "10, 12, 14, 16, 18, 20, ___?" This appears to be an example of a fully deterministic and fully predictable process, and a lot of our "predictions" about the future (e.g., that the sun will rise tomorrow) are like that. Without being able to make correct predictions on such matters, we would have a hard time surviving. In cases like the series above, we see a clear pattern, we posit a mechanism that produced it, and then we simply extrapolate to predict the next number. But while the next value in the sequence above might *seem* almost too obvious to talk about, when we are sure we know the answer, we are often fooling ourselves.

Since we are talking about *deterministic* processes, let's assume for the moment that the numbers in the sequence are not random and just happened to look so orderly. Even if the sequence truly is deterministic, it may be that our knowledge of the past sequence is too limited to really judge what is going on. Suppose, for example, that the full history of the sequence was "1, 2, 3, 4, 5, 6, 7, 8, 9, 10, 12, 14, 16, 18, 20." Now are you really sure that what comes next is actually 22? Sometimes a very simple straightforward deterministic process is actually very hard to predict.

In the land of determinism, this is only the beginning. It can get *much worse.*

In my childhood puzzle book, there were all sorts of clever and tricky patterns to discern. For example, there was the famous Fibonacci sequence where the rule was that each number was the sum of the last two numbers in the sequence—"1, 1, 2, 3, 5, 8, 13, 21, __?" Again, this is a fully deterministic sequence. In a way, it is more predictable than our first example since you don't need the full history to know what the next number is.

There are an almost infinite number of sequences like this with a multitude of different formulas to determine the sequences, enough to fill libraries full of puzzle books. Most of those "What comes next?" problems (as well as their real-life analogues) can be solved by our ingenious minds and by the even more ingenious computers. With enough numbers in the sequence, we can discern even highly complex patterns and make accurate predictions of future values. That is, of course, as we alluded to earlier, assuming you know enough of the past history of the sequence and that the future event that you are trying to predict is *in fact* the result of a deterministic process.

We are very good at finding patterns with our brains and with our learning machines, but I would argue that often we are *too* good at finding those patterns. All too often, we see deterministic order when we are actually looking at chaos or pure randomness that requires an entirely different set of tools to work with. Toward the end of this chapter, we will talk more about the philosophical implications of our plight, but for now, let's go back to some more "What comes next?" problems and look at chaos—a kind of no man's land that lies between the regions where determinism and randomness rule. It is a place where accurate short-term predictions are only approximate and long-term predictions are simply impossible.

Chaos: Deterministic but Not Predictable

In the middle of the last century, mathematicians and physicists all around the world, with the help of computers, almost simultaneously discovered the existence of chaos. There were many routes that those researchers took to find this heretofore hidden world. We will follow one of the more accessible trails to get there and begin with an examination of recursive sequences that can be produced in the following way:

(1) Take a number and do something to it; for example, multiply it by a factor and add it to another number.
(2) Then take the result and do *exactly* the same thing to it that you did to the first number (i.e., take the output of the process you have come up with and use it as the input for that same process).

What you get can then be looked at as one of the "What comes next?" problems we have been talking about. Some of the sequences have fascinating real-life manifestations. For example, the Fibonacci numbers can be used to derive the Golden Ratio that governs many biological processes we see all around us, including the number of petals on a flower, the shape of a snail shell, and the way pinecone seed pods arrange themselves.

With some ingenuity and persistence, almost all recursive sequences can be unraveled. However, there are some where the process produces a series of numbers that either requires an unreasonably large past history or an absolutely precise determination of each of the numbers in the sequence (i.e., number of decimals) to determine the next element in the series and where a long-term prediction is virtually impossible. Chaos is one of the most important types of those processes.

Most of the time, but not always, recursive processes produce sequences that are not only orderly but also either converge on a specific value, oscillate between several values, or blow up and get bigger and bigger. As mathematicians used their newly invented mainframe computers to explore these recursive sequences, they discovered that among the vast multitude of processes were some that produced an infinite string of numbers that had no discernable pattern whatsoever. This strange new world has no randomness in it, but unless you know the precise details of the process itself, but *the very first numbers in the sequence* (i.e., the initial conditions)as well, you can only make a good estimate of what comes next. Determining future values beyond the very near term with any accuracy is literally impossible. It was a staggering discovery whose philosophical implications we are still coming to grips with.

Chaos is a twilight zone where shadows and objects are indistinguishable. It is a place of mystery where an unseen algorithm creates the future in an inevitable but unknowable way. It is a path into the woods where the next few steps can be seen, but where the ultimate destination is shrouded in darkness. Fundamentally, it is a place where humans can only watch and wait for what comes next.

It turns out that even though it is hard to find a recursive process that has this magical quality, an uncomfortably large number of real-life processes are chaotic, perhaps even more than we suspect. Weather is a well-known example (it is literally impossible to accurately predict the weather on today's date a year from now), but it is also true that certain kinds of traffic jams and, even more troubling, the prices of many investments (e.g., commodities), and maybe even important measures of the economy are likely generated by a chaotic process.

The reason this last one is troubling is because a chaotic process can produce what *looks* like a pattern, and once that happens, armies of "market experts" arise to analyze the apparent patterns and begin to make economic/market predictions that, unless they are very short-term, almost always end up being wrong, sometimes catastrophically so.

In the face of these failures to predict, many economists and investment experts say that the market is not deterministic at all, but is a mix of determinism and randomness. Once that leap of faith is made, these experts then go on to say that because we understand randomness and probability theory, we can therefore make accurate long-term predictions (within certain ranges) by using sophisticated statistical tools and deep theoretical analysis of the random variables that govern markets and the economy in general. Putting aside the question of whether treating a (partially) deterministic process *as if* it were random can ever be useful, it turns out that the terrain of randomness is not quite as navigable as it first appears.

Randomland—An Untamed Wilderness

I just rolled a pair of dice twenty times, and here is what I got:

4, 7, 3, 10, 6, 6, 8, 5, 4, 7, 2, 7, 6, 10, 9, 6, 8, 9, 5, 7

Predicting what I will get if I roll the dice for the 21st time is another "What comes next?" problem. What is different about this one, however, is that because "the dice have no memory" and because I know *how* the numbers are produced (as long as the dice aren't loaded), I can ignore the results of those first twenty dice rolls. I know I can't predict *exactly* what the next number will be, but I *can* say something meaningful about what the next number will *probably* be.

For example, because I know details about the dice themselves, I know with absolute certainty that the next number *could* be any number from 2 through 12 (even though I didn't roll either an 11 or a 12). Furthermore, by *assuming* that my dice are fair, I can use basic probability theory to say that the expected value of the next number will be 7 and that there is a greater than 80 percent chance that the next number will be less than 10.

Rolling dice is an example of a "well-behaved" random process. We know the exact nature of the distribution of possible values, and because this is what is called a Gaussian distribution, we can make confident probabilistic predictions of what will happen in the future. From a technical point of view, this distribution is binomial. While I don't know what the next number will be, if I roll my dice a million more times, I will be able to predict quite accurately how many times I will get a 7 (a little more than 165,000 times), and I can be almost (but not quite) certain that, unlike the series above, I will get more 7s than 6s.

French mathematicians Blaise Pascal and Pierre de Fermat first discovered the rules of probability in 1654.[82] In addition to being a mathematician, Pascal was a gambler. The problem that Pascal and Fermat were trying to solve involved one of the most popular casino games being played then. It involved betting on how many rolls of a pair of dice were required before a 12 would come up. Not surprisingly, once he proved his new theorems, Pascal found himself not only unwelcome at the various gaming establishments in Paris, but he had also become a *persona non grata* in the eyes of the Church,[83] who viewed randomness as God's domain and thought that he and Fermat had obtained forbidden knowledge of the kind that would ultimately lead to humanity's downfall. Whether the Church was right is still an open question, but let's return now to our twenty dice rolls.

In the more than three hundred years since the discovery of probability theory, mathematicians have analyzed many other well-behaved probability distributions. Many of you who studied statistics in school might remember their esoteric names—Poisson, Student's t-distribution, Chi-squared test, and the ubiquitous normal distribution, among others. All of them share with the binomial distribution the very useful quality of allowing reasonably accurate predictions of the *range* of future outcomes, and all sorts of experts in a variety of fields from economics and medicine to sociology have (ab)used these distributions to make predictions and decisions that have large impacts on people's lives.

Most of the processes that experts make predictions about are far more complicated than rolling a pair of dice. Without knowing the actual mechanics of the process they are predicting, you might wonder how they know what distribution governs the variable they are trying to predict. The short answer is they don't, and that is the dirty little secret that no one talks about. Instead, what most experts do is look at a series of observations, like our twenty dice rolls above, and then make a judgment as to what kind of distribution best *fits the data*. Even worse, they choose a distribution (usually the normal distribution) because it is *easy* to perform the requisite calculations to make predictions. To be fair, there is a technical theoretical argument embodied in the Central Limit Theorem suggesting that many variables tend to be normally distributed, but even so, I still believe that the confidence that most experts place in their projections of the future is grossly misplaced. This is due to a number of factors.

First and foremost, even with the most sophisticated data mining techniques available today, it is not at all clear that enough data exists to ascertain the actual probability distribution governing the variable you are trying to predict (e.g., the future price of Exxon stocks). For example, while the distribution arising from my twenty dice roles is *consistent* with the binomial distribution it came from, unless I had a good independent reason to believe it was so, I couldn't be sure it was binomial. Even if I did make that assumption, based on the twenty data points I have, I might assume that my expected value was 6 and not 7 and that only values from 1 to 10 were possible. Even if I looked at 36 million dice rolls, it is highly unlikely that I would get *exactly* six million 7s (and one million 2s, two million 3s, etc.). In fact, the determination of what distribution governs a particular random variable is just an educated guess, and for reasons discussed quite clearly by Nassim Taleb and others, accurately determining a probability distribution by sampling can take *many* more observations than are generally available.[84] Beyond that, even if I have guessed correctly, what guarantee do I have that the distribution won't change over time, rendering all that historical data useless for determining the future?

There are even deeper problems with this approach. For understandable reasons, almost all of the guesses that experts make about the randomness governing what they are trying to predict is that it will be as well-behaved as that randomness governing my dice rolls. That means that they assume there will be a specific expected value (e.g., the expected value of rolling two dice is 7) and a specific variance (e.g., the amount by which the value might vary from the expected value). This might be convenient for the experts and comforting for those relying on the predictions, but the landscape of randomness is wild, and there are many distributions where, even though we might be able to determine an expected value, the potential range by which we could be wrong is almost infinite. There are even some where *both* the expected value and its potential range of variance are *much larger* than what you might guess from just looking at historical data. As weird as the concept might sound, evidence is accumulating that some of the most important variables, particularly economic ones, are governed by these unruly distributions.

Fat Tails and Black Swans

Most of us are familiar with the 80/20 rule. This is also known as the Pareto Principle, named for the Italian civil engineer Vilfredo Pareto who observed in 1906 that 80 percent of the land in Italy was owned by 20 percent of the population.[85] Its applicability seems to be ubiquitous in our lives, from crime statistics (where well over 80 percent of the country's murders occur in 20 percent of the counties) to business (where 80 percent of many companies' revenue come from 20 percent of their customers). The 80/20 rule is especially prominent when it comes to economic measures, where well over 80 percent of the world's wealth is owned by 20 percent of the population.

This might be only a curious phenomenon and a good topic for cocktail conversation, except that when the 80/20 rule governs a random variable, it is indicative of what is known as a fat-tailed distribution, which are decidedly *not* well-behaved. Consider, for example, the distribution of wealth in the US. The average net worth of an American household is $692,000. If I were to look at a random sample of twenty households, I might find that ten of them have less than $100,000, another six have between $100,000 and $500,000, three have around $1,000,000 in assets, and then one outlier has anywhere from $5,000,000 to $100,000,000,000 in net worth. If I were to then calculate the "sample mean" of those twenty, I could get almost any number from much less than the average of $692,000 to something much greater. Now, if we think about those twenty households as a "What comes next?" problem, we can see that we really can't say anything meaningful about the next number in the series, unless we knew the total wealth distribution from which our samples were pulled.

Nassim Taleb has written extensively about fat tails, and in particular, has argued quite convincingly that much of the investment world (including the stock market) is governed by fat-tailed distributions rather than normal distribution as most financial planners would have you believe. In the next chapter, we will look at Taleb's math in greater detail and discuss how to use his insights about fat tails to develop a financial strategy that you may want to consider.

More generally, the question is, what do we do when we are confronted with a "What comes next?" problem that may arise from a fat-tailed distribution? The first and most important caution is *don't ignore that outlier in the series*. There is a great temptation to consider that billionaire we happened to pick as an aberration or a noise in the process that can be safely ignored. However, it is exactly the possibility of the low probability/high impact event that we need to be attentive to when we are considering the future. Taleb calls these events "black swans" because, just like the black swans discovered in Australia after millions of white swans were observed in Europe, black swan events are those that have never happened before and were assumed to be impossible. The critical point is that, "absence of evidence is not evidence of absence."

The second, and almost equally important conclusion to draw when you suspect that the future you are needing to predict is governed by a fat-tailed distribution, is to not rely too much on past history to make decisions for the future. Focus more on what the underlying process *might* be, rather than assume what it *is*. When it comes to investing your money, this is a very difficult advice to follow, and requires a great deal more sophistication and utilization of optionality than most people are prepared to engage in. As Bernie Madoff, the Great Depression, and the financial crisis of 2008–2009 all demonstrated, though, black swans do occur, and those who do not consider the possibility of them can be ruined financially.

Here Be Dragons

I wish that were the end of the story. Unfortunately, there are regions of Randomland where we know even less than we do under fat-tailed distributions, like the randomness governing the distribution of wealth in the US. Under these kinds of distributions, the past only provides limited insight to the future. In particular, determining the shape of the distribution (i.e., how "fat" the tail is) sometimes requires knowing almost the entire range of possible outcomes (e.g., when we talked about the wealth distribution of the US). Even so, there we could at least make *some* statements about what the future might look like. A typical fat-tailed distribution does have an expected value that can shed light on a "What comes next?" problem based on such a distribution.

However, mathematicians have discovered that there are other probability distributions where *both* the expected value and the variance by which that value might diverge are undeterminable. They are called "Pareto Type I with alpha = 1" distributions, and if you are faced with one of these, there is absolutely nothing meaningful you can say about the future. You can't even say, based on even an arbitrarily long past history, whether or not you are embedded in one. Because of the above, we have no idea if anything in the real world is governed by such a distribution; their theoretical existence adds a final dimension to the uncertainty that we live in.

In the Jewish tradition, there are many ways to refer to God, from the mundane "Elohim" which refers to all the unseen workings of nature and "Adonai," where the more ephemeral aspects of the human spirit reside, all the way to the ultimate "Ein Sof," which is not a name per se, but rather a Hebrew word that means endless or infinite. To me, it is inspiring to think that, as clever as we are, thinking we have surveyed the world of uncertainty, there are still parts that we will never know. The ancients were aware of this, and assumed that monsters lived in the unknown expanses of the world that had not yet been explored. They knew that when venturing into those regions, they needed to be well-equipped and well-armed, but they also knew that in the end, only luck, courage, and the ability to adapt quickly to whatever they encountered would ensure their survival.

In today's world, our maps may be more precise and our weapons more sophisticated, but when you travel in the land of Uncertainty, it is important to have the right mindset—to be fearless, curious, and flexible. In a world that is ever-changing, this is an aspect of the human condition that hasn't changed in thousands of years and is highly unlikely to change any time soon.

Chapter 8
Fat Tails, Black Swans, and Buying Barbells

As I said in the Introduction, I tend to be very risk-averse, particularly when it comes to my job. From the time I graduated from college in 1979 until the middle of 1998, I worked for big companies with long histories of stability and profitability. I never changed jobs until I had a guaranteed offer in hand from another company. I never burned bridges with prior employers; I always gave plenty of notice and strictly adhered to non-compete and non-disclosure agreements that I willingly signed. I strove to be a model employee and was rewarded with good salaries, decent bonuses, and almost complete job security. I never took a chance with my paycheck.

But in 1998, I took a leap of entrepreneurial faith and agreed to become a partner with James Kenney at his firm Coates Kenney, a small boutique actuarial firm in Berkeley. Kenney had taken over the firm from the founder Barrett Coates a few years earlier after Barrett had retired and then tragically died shortly after. Kenney is a spectacularly good actuary, but didn't like wearing suits or going to client meetings. He preferred to sit in his office working at his computer wearing jeans and a tie-dyed T-shirt while Keith Jarret or the Grateful Dead blared from the stereo system he had installed shortly after Barrett retired. The firm was profitable enough, but most of the revenue came from two large corporate clients that all the big consulting firms were constantly trying to steal. In short, Kenney needed help and offered me the opportunity to join him in a business whose future was clearly governed by one of those fat-tailed distributions we just discussed.

I can't say that I accepted the offer because I did a thorough and robust analysis. In fact, all I did was look closely enough to see that *if* we could hold on to our two main clients, I would make much more money than I ever had before. If we didn't, I would shortly be out of a job. I also really liked Kenney and it seemed like it would be a lot of fun, no matter what happened.

The fact is, from a professional and financial perspective, my decision worked out far better than I could have expected. This is a great example of the upside potential of exposing yourself to a fat-tailed distribution. Of course, things might have worked out differently—I could have found myself unemployed, and the risk I took with my career could have led to financial disaster. If I had to do it again, I probably would still have taken the chance, but I would have considered my choice as an "option" and incorporated it into a broader "barbell strategy," which we will talk about below.

Before talking about optionality and the idea of a barbell strategy, we first need to talk about two other critical concepts discussed by Nassim Taleb. The first is path dependence,[86] a concept that everyone understands but most people rarely consider. Fundamentally, it means that when imagining different aspects of your possible future (e.g., the value of your house in ten years), it is important to consider the path that leads to that future. So, for example, suppose you decide to invest $150,000 in a house worth $500,000. You take out a new thirty-year $350,000 mortgage requiring a loan and property tax payment of $3,000 per month (about equal, net of taxes, to what you might have to pay in rent). Your net equity is therefore $150,000. If everything goes as planned and the house appreciates at a steady 4 percent per year, you could end up with a house worth about $740,000 after ten years, with a loan balance of a little bit less than $300,000. It will increase your net equity to $440,000, a very nice return on your initial $150,000.

However, there are two problems with that scenario. First, what if instead of rising steadily at 4 percent per year, the road is "choppier"? Say, the housing market drops 25 percent in the first year and then goes up and down with returns averaging 7.2 percent per year for the next nine years (still an average of 4 percent per year). In that case, rather than being worth $740,000, your house will only be worth less than $700,000 (perhaps much less depending on how volatile those returns are during the nine years). But even assuming a steady 7.2 percent return during the nine years, the ten-year annualized return on your investment has gone from 11.4 percent to 10.3 percent. Actuaries call this phenomenon "sequence of returns risk." In this case, it has only made a superlative investment a little less spectacular, but in other cases, it can make the difference between a winning and a losing strategy.

There is a much more important aspect of path dependence that needs to be highlighted. Specifically, note that in the example above, we have assumed a 25 percent drop in the housing market in the first year. What if that drop was the result of a serious downturn in the economy? And what if some of the fallout from that downturn was that you lost your job and couldn't afford to make the mortgage payments? Now you will have to sell your house (currently worth $375,000 after the drop) and will be left with a mere $25,000 after paying off the $350,000 you still owe. The return on your $150,000 investment has been a catastrophic negative 83.3 percent, and your chances of accumulating your expected $400,000-plus payoff after ten years have receded into insignificance.

This is an example of fragility, and it is very much related to the fragility we discussed in Chapter 1. In that chapter, we defined a system (or individual) as fragile if they were harmed by volatility and said that Taleb's term "antifragile" was the opposite; that is, Taleb's system benefits from volatility. Now I want to get a little more precise about both fragility and anti-fragility.

Specifically, an investment (or any system for that matter) is fragile if its response to stressors (e.g., the effect of volatility in the economy on your net home equity in the example above) is non-linear, and in particular, concave down. You can see this in your house investment by noting that even if the relationship between the economy and housing prices was linear, the downturn in the economy that caused a 25 percent drop in housing prices would have caused more than twice as much damage to your investment as a downturn only half as bad causing only a 12.5

percent drop in housing prices (upon the sale, you would have been left with $87,500, or more than three times as much as if prices had dropped 25 percent). But it is even worse than that. If the economic downturn had been milder, you might not have lost your job, thus allowing you to "stay in the game" and continue to make your mortgage payments until housing prices recovered. In *Antifragile*, Taleb considers many examples of things (including investments, ecologies, corporate, political, and financial systems, among others) that are fragile, as well as other systems that are antifragile, where stressors produce a convex up response and disproportionate returns are experienced (or strengthened) as the environment gets more variable.

One very important aspect of antifragility is that, unlike fragility, it entails optionality and asymmetry. The optionality (on investments, for example) comes from having many "irons in the fire," some of which can be pulled from the fire at any time. Asymmetry, on the other hand, comes from having a limited and finite downside with an upside that is either unlimited or unknown, but potentially far in excess of the amount of the downside. With having many small "bets" in play, no single one can be expected to pay off, but if from the many, one or a few *do* pay off, the returns should be so disproportionately positive as to outweigh the small individual losses that all the other investments might experience before the payoff arrives. In fact, if not for the possibility that none of the many little long shot investments will pay off, leaving you with big or maybe total losses, then investing all your assets in an antifragile manner might make sense as a personal investing strategy. As we will discuss in the final section of this book, that kind of strategy runs counter to the basic idea of Holistic Financial Wellness where so many components are interrelated and failures can cascade. As a result, when one's total financial picture (including your future and the fragilities that arise from these interdependencies) is taken into account, it is clear that another strategy is indicated, not just for investing, but for the overall management of your financial life.

Simply stated, a barbell strategy is one that is simultaneously extremely conservative and extremely aggressive. It protects against those aspects of your financial situation that are fragile and takes advantage of the convex returns for those aspects of your financial situation that can be isolated and made antifragile. The math is complicated, but, fundamentally, this kind of strategy can work whenever the situation you are applying it to is a complex non-linear system and can be separated into components. As I have written elsewhere, the core insights of Holistic Financial Wellness arose because of the complex interactions between the various interdependent components of our financial worlds. In addition to being complex, the consequences of our financial decisions, as shown above, are very often decidedly non-linear. It is also true, as we see below, that some sections of your financial life can be "cordoned off" and treated separately.

Taleb's Math and Some Cautions about Fat Tails

Nassim Taleb is not a very nice man, and he admits it.[87] However, he is masterful when it comes to statistical analysis. If you can tolerate his arrogance (I actually find it entertaining), you will find his books full of insights and helpful advice. His most accessible book is *Fooled by Randomness* but his best is *Antifragile*. Both can be completely understood by anyone who has understood and appreciated the first seven chapters of this book. That being said, neither of his books are about math, per se. While I have become a believer in his view of the world of uncertainty, I was not fully convinced until I went through his most recent book, *Statistical Consequences of Fat Tails*. In that book, Taleb lays out the mathematical underpinnings for his many provocative pronouncements. What he demonstrates about the fat-tailed distributions that govern so much of our economic life is eye-opening, to say the least.

Throughout this book as well as in *What's Your Future Worth?*[88] I have discussed the importance and the challenges of estimating the probability of certain outcomes (e.g., that you will earn at least 7 percent per year if you invest in the stock market). We noted in Chapter 7 that many of the random variables that drive such outcomes are not normally distributed as some investment experts would have you believe. Instead, they are subject to much greater variability and emerge from distributions that have fat tails. A fat-tailed distribution simply means a probability distribution where instances that are very unlikely to occur (i.e., from the tail of the distribution) have a disproportionate impact on your expected value. We discussed this earlier when we talked about the distribution of wealth among the population. There, we saw how the impact of a few billionaires could distort the average American's net worth.

To expand on the challenge of dealing with a fat-tailed distribution, consider meeting a random stranger and guessing what their net worth is. If you used the expected value (i.e., the *mean*), you would guess the amount to be about $700,000. On the other hand, if you used the *median* amount of household wealth (i.e., the amount that 50 percent of the population have, more or less), the figure is only $97,300. This huge difference between the mean and the median is characteristic of a fat-tailed distribution. It makes it treacherous to make financial decisions based on expected values where you are assuming the probability of the variable you are dealing with is governed by a normal distribution, where the mean and the median tend to be pretty close to each other.

You may be asking, if we know the distribution is fat-tailed (not always so easy to figure out), couldn't we simply recalculate the probabilities, considering the shape of the distribution? The answer is "Maybe." But as Taleb demonstrates compellingly, it is much harder than it looks because of one aspect of these kinds of distributions that almost no expert will admit to. While almost any good statistician can calculate the mean, median, and standard deviation of a probability distribution if they know the precise shape of the distribution (as well as other key parameters), the challenge is how to know the specific type of distribution you are dealing with. That is where most experts fail to heed Taleb's math.

If you look closely at what virtually every expert says, you will see that the distributions they assume are based on historical data. Sometimes that data is extensive. For example, estimates about expected returns and standard deviation for stock portfolios are based on what the stock market has done over the many years that we have been keeping records. Unfortunately, in almost all cases where a fat-tailed distribution is involved, there is *simply not enough data to determine with any confidence what the shape of the distribution is.* This is a powerful and discouraging result, but Taleb demonstrates this inconvenient truth compellingly and mathematically. The fact that he berates and ridicules his naysayers unmercifully is, in my view, irrelevant. It is simply one of the "statistical consequences of fat tails."

Now, as much of a supporter of Taleb's view as I am, I do believe he sometimes goes too far in his criticism of others who work in the field of risk evaluation. While he has never attacked me or my actuarial colleagues for misunderstanding risk, I also don't think he has given us enough credit. Actuaries do understand fat-tailed distributions. Over the years, we have learned to both respect them and to glean what bits of information *are possible* to gather when you are dealing with a random variable that can be dangerous to your health—financial and otherwise. There is now an entire branch of actuarial science—Extreme Value Theory[89]—devoted to managing such risks. Extreme Value Theory is used by insurance companies that issue insurance on catastrophic risks of all kinds. While one day the fat tail of one of those distributions might whip around and badly damage one of those companies, the actuaries on watch will not be surprised. They will almost certainly have taken steps to keep their company from going out of business.

Your job, however, is much simpler. All you need to do is ensure your own survival in the financial world where fat tails cannot just bankrupt you, but also allow you to become financially secure.

Let's see what I mean.

An Example of a Barbell Strategy in Holistic Financial Wellness

In addition to being a brilliant thinker when it comes to uncertainty and risk, Taleb is also a philosopher with both a well-articulated view on ethics and a fairly unique perspective on the relationship between theory and practice. In particular, he believes strongly that practice informs theory and not the other way around. Related to this is his view that one should reject anyone who offers advice or takes action that will affect others when they don't have any skin in the game. I fully agree with him on this point, and therefore the barbell strategy I want to talk about is one that I have taken in my own life.

In 2016, after almost forty years of working in the retirement plan industry, I retired from my employer. I then had to sit down and figure out how to manage life (financial and otherwise) without the benefit of an organization to provide me with work to do every day and money to live on. I thought I was prepared for it, but as with most things, reality is somewhat different from theory. On paper, I had done all the right things; I saved an adequate amount each year, invested in a balanced portfolio (although I am sure my asset allocation was not on the "efficient frontier"), and managed my debt and annual expenses in such a way that theoretically all my future liabilities could be met by income from my savings and the pensions I had earned along the way. But the more I looked at things from a holistic point of view, the more I saw how fragile my financial life actually was. There were all kinds of systemic risks and potential fragilities I hadn't analyzed in detail, from the possibility that I might live far beyond my life expectancy, to the possibility that there might be an economic discontinuity that could cause the market(s) to crash and/or double-digit inflation and interest rates to return. There were local disasters (e.g., earthquakes) and global catastrophes (e.g., war or a financial system collapse), which would have both first- and second-order financial effects to consider. Any one of these disasters was a low likelihood event, but as Taleb points out, not only does it take only one to wreak havoc with your plans, but eventually, one of these black swan events is inevitable, and time itself is a source of volatility. The long period over which I expected to be retired made a seriously concave result that is something to consider and protect against.

In the end, I decided to go against conventional wisdom and the advice put forth by the most sophisticated retirement planners. I embarked on my own barbell strategy. I sunk almost 75 percent of my retirement assets into the purchase of guaranteed lifetime annuities, TIPS (Treasury Inflation-Protected Security), and gold. When I get a little older (I'm only 64), I will also take out a reverse mortgage credit line on our house to provide additional cushion against catastrophes. This ultra-conservative end of the barbell strategy will provide enough to live on if even the worst happens. The rest I have broken up into small pieces. I am investing in highly speculative ventures (e.g., leveraged rental income units in gentrifying neighborhoods with non-recourse financing, some small cap equities, and a few other investments in unconventional long shots like old books and collectibles) to form the other end of the barbell.

Unfortunately, I didn't have enough hard assets to create a truly balanced barbell, but as I thought more holistically about my financial life, I realized that the other investable assets I have are my time and earnings capacity (retirement planners almost never tell you that this is the third most valuable asset most retirees own after their home and their retirement savings). With that time, I am adding to the second side of the barbell by involving myself in several "fixed downside/unbounded upside" ventures that I enjoy and could have possible but unknown financial upsides for me. I may talk about some of those other antifragile ventures in a later piece as many of them also provide non-financial upsides (e.g., writing and speaking about Holistic Financial Wellness). It will give me an opportunity to discuss some of the other more complex concepts that Taleb addresses in his work.

As I write these words, I continue to be unwavering in my faith in both the unknowability of the future and our ability as humans to survive and even thrive in that uncertainty. I truly believe that all we need to do is accept that uncertainty is an immutable reality and move as quickly as we can from the fragile to the antifragile. As Taleb says, "The tragedy is that much of what you think is random is in your control, and what's worse, the opposite."[90] The trick is knowing the difference between the two.

In light of the above, it is vital to not only have the right strategy to thrive in an uncertain world, but also to have the right attitude to do so. We now turn to the question of *practical* risk management in the financial world.

Chapter 9
Making Smart Bets—Getting Comfortable with Not Knowing

About thirty years ago, my father and I decided to hike and camp in the Sawtooth Mountains of Idaho. Since neither of us had the skills nor the experience to survive in this kind of wilderness, we hired a professional, Dave Bingham,[91] to show us the way and to make sure we didn't get lost or worse. Beyond competent, Dave had a calm positive energy that made my dad and I feel both safe and adventurous. We followed Dave deep into the mountains, trekking a dozen miles each day, as he led us to pristine alpine lakes where we would catch trout for dinner and camp for the night. It was a wonderful trip and a source of great memories, but it was also a trip where I came face to face with questions that I still constantly ponder.

Throughout the day, Dave took good care of us and made sure we didn't get into trouble. However, he also needed some alone time. Every evening after cleaning up, while my father and I struggled to set up our tent, Dave would head up to one of the nearby peaks and do a little free climbing, arriving back in camp just before the sun set. The first couple of days, my Dad and I were too distracted by our struggles with the tent to notice where he was going, but on the third day, we spied him scrambling up an impossibly steep cliff about 500 yards away. Watching his progress through our binoculars, we stared in fascinated horror as Dave climbed higher and higher—without ropes or a partner—up to heights where any slip would be catastrophic, leaving him broken and us stranded in the wilderness. This was risk-taking far beyond anything I had witnessed in my career as an actuary. I simply could not understand why or how someone would act so cavalierly with no apparent awareness of the possible consequences of their behavior.

When Dave returned to camp, refreshed and only slightly winded, we sat him down for a serious talk. I started by asking why he took such an incredible risk with his life and our well-being. He didn't seem to understand the question, and so my father tried a different tack. First, he asked Dave what probability did he think there was of him falling and dying when he set out. He simply shrugged, said he hadn't really thought about it but was very comfortable on the rocks. He said that he had no doubt that he would get down safely as he had done similar climbs hundreds of times before and never had a problem. Seeing that Dave still wasn't getting it, my father posed a different question:

"Suppose you *knew* that you had a one in a thousand chance of falling and dying, would you still climb that peak?"

"Oh sure," he said.

"What if the chances were one in five hundred?"

"No problem," he replied immediately.

Now my father was getting concerned that we were in the hands of a lunatic and that *our* chances of getting back in one piece were less than he had originally thought.

When he next asked, "How about one in one hundred?" Dave finally paused and said, "Well, maybe if it was *that* risky, I would reconsider."

At that point, we dropped the subject. We did spend much of the next few days contemplating the implications of the discussion, and the many other unknown (and maybe unknowable) aspects of the spectacularly high stakes gambling that we had witnessed.

What were Dave's actual chances of falling on that climb? What was his pay-off for making the successful climb, and was it really a smart bet for Dave? How should all the other costs and benefits of the bet be incorporated into Dave's decision? For example, how did he view the risk to us of his failure? How much value did Dave put on the rest of his future life versus the immediate pleasure and benefit he would get by climbing up and down? To what extent were there benefits beyond the immediate pleasure he would receive by "winning" his bet and getting up and down the cliff safely? That is, might he also be seeking knowledge of the terrain, practicing additional skills to use for the next climb, or maybe just seeking some other kind of self-knowledge that is only accessible when you are standing on top of a high, isolated cliff in the middle of Idaho? And then there was perhaps the biggest question of all—what kind of attitude allowed Dave to be so comfortable with the uncertain and potentially cataclysmic future that he was inviting into his life with the decision to climb that cliff?

Neither my father nor I could make any headway with this last question. While I have pondered it periodically in the years since I returned from Idaho, I still haven't made much progress. Yet, it is, in some ways, the fundamental question we have to ask ourselves each time we make a decision, financial or otherwise, that entails the possibility of some painful (or worse) consequence that may occur if the outcome of our decision is not what we hope.

Fortunately, there *are* people who can provide insights about this question. Recently, I had the opportunity to talk with someone who is an expert at making good bets and who has learned, over many years, how to be comfortable when the stakes are high and the outcome highly uncertain.

In 1992, Annie Duke was at Penn University, well on her way to becoming a Ph.D. in Cognitive Psychology,[92] when she discovered that her basic math aptitude, deep theoretical knowledge of human behavior, and desire to operationalize her insights were the perfect prerequisites for a much more lucrative career—that of a professional poker player. For the next twenty years, Annie played at the highest level of the game, placing first in the 2004 World Series of Poker Tournament of Champions and becoming the first and only woman ever to win the National Heads-Up Poker Championship.[93] She has collected over $4 million in winnings during her career and has demonstrated, in a statistically significant way, that she knows how to make good bets.

In 2018, Annie decided to share her way of thinking with the world and published *Thinking in Bets*,[94] a book that is, in my view, one of the best and most practical ever written on how to make decisions under uncertainty. While not specifically about financial decisions, and in particular, the long-term decisions that are most critical to ensuring enduring financial wellness, Annie's insights about the nature of uncertainty and the mental mindset we should be adopting when facing the unknown (and unknowable) future are well worth considering.

When I reached out to Annie and told her that I was in the process of writing a book addressing a similar topic, she graciously agreed to share her perspective on the application of her expertise to the specific problems associated with financial planning, most particularly how to thrive in a world full of unknowns.

In *Thinking in Bets*, Annie says, "What good poker players and good decision makers have in common is their comfort with the world being an uncertain and unpredictable place."[95] Perhaps that is obvious, but what Annie says next is very important and potentially counterintuitive, or at least unnatural, for most of us. She says that to make good decisions, it is important for people to "figure out how *unsure* they are" and to "make their best guess at the chances that different outcomes will occur."

Annie believes that all decisions are "bets," and the same thinking that leads to making smart bets will also lead to making good decisions. I agree completely, and there are many similarities. There are also some important differences among the kinds of bets that Annie is most concerned with and the financial decisions that we have been discussing throughout this book.

First, let's look at some similarities and how Annie's insights can be helpful to maintain your financial health.

In the last two chapters, we discussed the nature of uncertainty in the context of how events (deterministic, chaotic, or random) transform the present into the future, but there is another aspect to uncertainty that we have neglected to mention but which Annie takes on directly. Specifically, we often need to make decisions when we have *incomplete information about the current situation*. In poker, this arises because we don't know the unseen cards that the other players hold and can only make educated guesses about what they might be based on other information (e.g., what bets they have made earlier in the hand, what facial expressions they may be wearing, the basic probability of specific card holdings, and a host of other indirect clues). The same is true for most of the financial decisions that we must make. One of the reasons Annie is so good at what she does is that she is able to quickly analyze these clues to make a better guess about the unknown information. While she won't know until the hand is over whether or not her deductions were correct, evaluating and getting comfortable with this kind of uncertainty is just as important as learning to live with the randomness of what the future holds.

In evaluating incomplete information, knowing probability theory is of limited value. Guesses about the unseen cards based on indirect clues (as distinct from the *a priori* probability that an opponent holds a certain card) are either right or wrong. It is our *internal* processes for developing those guesses that are most important to hone here, rather than an ability to understand and calculate probabilities.

I think some of Dave Bingham's confidence about free climbing up the cliffs of Idaho comes from his ability to be comfortable with this latter kind of uncertainty. Dave believed (perhaps correctly) that the biggest uncertainty in climbing is associated with an incomplete understanding of both the cliff itself and his own physical capabilities to ascend the peak. To an observer trying to evaluate the probability of a climber falling, these two sources of uncertainty can become conflated. For example, in considering the frequency of rock-climbing accidents, it is virtually impossible to distinguish between climbers who simply made bad guesses about the unknown and those who fell because of a completely random gust of wind or muscle spasm. This may have been why it was so hard for Dave to understand and respond to our questions. Not only did he think that he had eliminated all the uncertainty associated with both the mountain and his own capabilities, he simply didn't think the residual uncertainty associated with randomness was that important. Perhaps he was right, but I also don't think that Dave understood probability theory or the fact that if you take a 1/500 risk one hundred times in a row, you only have an 80 percent chance of surviving the experience.

Fortunately, Annie Duke does understand how to factor in probability theory, and more importantly, how to separate the unpredictability of future outcomes from the incomplete information that can be an equal, if not greater, source of uncertainty in every decision we make, financial or otherwise. As a poker player, she also didn't just rely on her experience (or deep pattern recognition skills) to become a champion. Instead, she actively tried to get better at making guesses about incomplete information. Since almost none of us will make enough financial decisions in our lives to develop the intuition for the unseen cards that Annie undoubtedly has, it is those techniques for educating our guesses that are important to master.

We will talk more in the next section about how Annie's insights on how the challenges posed by our internal biases and cognitive limitations can be taken on directly. By overcoming our inherent irrationality, we can train ourselves to learn to make better guesses about the unseen aspects of the financial choices we face. For now, however, let's simply listen to what she says about the attitude one should have when dealing with incomplete information.

According to Annie, one of the biggest hurdles we need to overcome when facing a decision where we have incomplete information is not that we don't know everything we need to know. Rather, it is the *belief* we already have about the hidden information. As Annie says, "We don't recognize how flimsy the foundation is for many of our beliefs."[96] This is as true when facing an important financial decision as it is when trying to figure out the cards that your opponents are holding in a high-stakes game of poker.

Let's say, for example, that your career is starting to take off and you are earning much more money than you are spending. As you think about this discretionary income, you try to decide whether to put more money into your 401(k) and other retirement savings or to use a portion of your accumulated assets for a down payment on a second home where you and your family can spend your vacation. You recognize that if you are going to buy another house, your new mortgage payments will reduce your ability to save more. On the other hand, you also recognize that not only is a second home an investment, having this home will also provide you with non-monetary benefits both in the short and long term.

You face a complex and important financial decision where there is a great deal of uncertainty about the future outcome of this investment.

As an investment, you need, among other things, to assess whether the vacation home will appreciate at a rate greater than what you can earn on your 401(k) investments. Beyond its financial return, you need to recognize that the mortgage debt you assume to buy the house will add a degree of leverage that will increase the stakes of the bet; that is, the return on your net investment will be amplified by the fact that your purchase will add *both* an asset and a liability to your personal balance sheet. You also need to assess how the assumption of a significant amount of long-term debt will affect your future financial situation.

Will it make you fragile in the way we discussed earlier? Will it prevent you from taking advantage of other better investment opportunities that may come your way? There are other questions you should also be asking yourself. For example, will your income continue at a level high enough to accommodate two house payments? What other lifestyle or career opportunities will you be forgoing as a result of committing such a large percentage of your investable resources? Will you and your family continue to want to vacation in the same place every year now that you have no (economic) reason to go elsewhere? Will your future health and lifestyle allow you to get the full enjoyment out of the house in the future? These are just some of the uncertainties about the future that you will have to address.

The above questions all relate to uncertainty about the future, but there is also a great deal about the *current* situation that is likely unknown to you and needs attention. This is often an underappreciated aspect of financial planning where Annie's techniques can be of great assistance.

For example, let's say you live in San Francisco. You want to buy that vacation home near Lake Tahoe where you and your family have enjoyed many vacations. Every year on the drive up, you pass through quaint little mountain towns and you tell yourself, each time, how nice it would be to own a place in one of those communities. You imagine being able to go at any time of the year with no advance planning. You tell yourself that the financial risk is minimal because, if necessary, you can rent the house out while you aren't using it, and it really should not be viewed as negatively impacting your retirement savings. The house itself could even serve as a spot to retire to in the future. Let's say you have even spent some time in the towns you are considering and have met with a local real estate agent to get a sense of the market and what the numbers might look like.

But, with all that you know (or think that you know) do you really understand what it is like to own property in the community you will be joining? What are the neighbors like? What about the politics? Beyond the unknown future, there are a lot of other things you don't know about what you might be buying *right now*. As with any investment, buying a second home requires due diligence. The path toward uncovering the hidden downsides (and upsides) about a given property and the mortgage you take on it is well-trodden, but what about the aspects of the purchase that you *believe* you already know? For example, you might have heard from the real estate agent that the rental market is strong and if you had to, you could rent your new home to help meet the mortgage payments if you ever ran into financial difficulties. Is that really true? What kind of permits are required if you want to turn your place into an Airbnb? What kind of taxes and management fees would be required, and how long would it take to get your place ready to rent if you had to do so?

And then there is your belief about yourself. You may be thinking that you might want to retire in Lake Tahoe, so the home can be part of a larger retirement planning strategy, but is that really true? In *Thinking in Bets*, Annie tells a wonderful story of a high-stakes gambler who bet a friend $30,000 that he could live in De Moines, Iowa for thirty days without going crazy.[97] Being an experienced gambler, he had well analyzed what he thought were all the angles of the proposition. He analyzed how much in gambling income he would be losing by being out of Las Vegas for a month, what, if any, potential additional skills in other games like pool or golf he could develop with his time off that could generate additional gambling income when he returned, and many other variables. Only, he had neglected to analyze the most fundamental variable of all—whether or not he could actually tolerate living in such a quiet town for that long. As Annie points out, "In most of our decisions, we are not betting against another person. Rather, we are betting against all the future versions of ourselves that we are not choosing."[98]

We will have a lot more to say in Chapter 12 about how to learn to make better guesses about the unseen cards that are associated with most of our financial decisions and our tendency to let our biases and cognitive blocks lead us astray. Before we get there, we will conclude this chapter with an important distinction between playing poker and making important personal financial decisions.

Making Big Long-Term Bets

There is one aspect of financial decision-making that is somewhat different from playing poker. Professional poker players like Annie make tens of thousands of bets every year, and as long as she consistently makes good bets, at the end of the day (or year), she is very likely to come out ahead. Unfortunately, most of us have far fewer opportunities in our financial lives to make the "right" choice, and even worse, the consequences of each of our choices tend to be much greater than a simple poker hand. Sometimes the stakes are so high that even if you make a "smart" bet, the impact on your financial health can be disastrous if it comes out badly—so bad that you don't have time to recover.

In my business, ironically enough, this is called the "gambler's ruin problem," and actuaries stay up late into the night thinking about this issue as they help insurance companies set underwriting and pricing standards (our form of betting) so that a series of unlucky claims will not bankrupt their employer. In *Thinking in Bets*, Annie discusses "resulting"[99] and how we should never judge the quality of our decisions by their results. When everything is riding on the result of a single bet, knowing you made the right decision even though the result was catastrophic is of small comfort.

When I brought this to Annie's attention, she readily agreed and said that the issue I raised is akin to the "all-in" bet that one sometimes has to make in poker, where an opponent makes a bet so large that in order to continue the hand, you have to put all your money into the pot. If you lose, you are out of the game. If you win, you get to keep playing.

As a general rule, Annie advises minimizing the likelihood that you will be faced with such a situation. She recommends various techniques to do that, the most applicable of which (for our purposes) is effective money management. You limit the size of your bets to a small enough proportion of your assets so that you don't find yourself in such a situation. This might seem like obvious advice when it comes to making financial decisions that could bankrupt you, but it is surprising how easily we are seduced by the possibility of a substantial upside with a seemingly modest downside, without considering the worst-case scenario where you lose your entire investment. If the investment is a large enough percentage of your assets, you need to consider this an all-in bet even if the probability of losing it all seems very small.

Because of the above, we make all-in bets more often than we think. We would all do well to heed Annie's advice when she says that in poker, "even though you can't always avoid an 'all-in' bet, you can often make it a mathematical mistake for your opponent to make you go all in." In other words, when the decision is really high stakes, you want to make sure that the odds are as stacked in your favor as they can possibly be. But Annie also acknowledges that when the stakes are high enough and the consequences of failure severe enough, just trying to make "the percentage play" is not sufficient. Since it is always possible to "fold" and not make the all-in bet, we need to go further and evaluate our tolerance for risk.

We have talked about this in prior chapters. In fact, principle #5 speaks directly to the objective aspects of this point where we state that becoming antifragile is critical to maintaining financial health. In the last chapter, we talked about barbell strategies designed not only to provide you with more upside potential than downside on an ongoing basis, but to protect you as well from financial ruin if an aspect of your financial situation or the markets you are invested in suddenly collapses. When facing a really important financial decision, it is important not to get *too* focused on the probabilities and expected value of the decision/ bet you are about to make, but rather, to stay aware of your own feelings about the risk of a catastrophe that, like a fall from an Idaho cliff, can put you out of the game.

In addition to the higher stakes associated with each individual financial decision, there is another subtler difference between a poker bet and the choices we make in our financial lives. Specifically, the outcomes of investment, career, and retirement planning choices are usually much further in the future than in a poker game where the next turn of the card will take place in minutes, rather than the years it will often take to know whether our financial decisions have turned out well. What this means, for our purposes, is that to truly know whether we are making a good or bad financial decision, we need to have a full awareness of our "time preference."

The concept of time preference was first formalized by Irving Fisher,[100] a famous economist who, in the early 1900s, first recognized and tried to incorporate the impact of how *much* people preferred current versus future consumption into economic theory. Note that this individual preference is very different from the objective discount rate that finance professionals use to compare the value of assets and liabilities where the cash income (or outflow) will vary over time. That rate is a function of investment returns and the probability of future contingencies that might affect future cash flow. As an actuary, the notion of a discount rate is critical to all that I do, and the concept of determining the value today of what will happen in the future—that is, determining the *actuarial present value*, is in some ways the essence of actuarial work. The science of determining present value is well-established for economic entities, but as we are talking here about making *individual* financial decisions, we need to combine time preference and actuarial present value. Only by doing so can we determine an appropriate personal discount rate to use in making better (for us) financial decisions.

It is a formidable, and largely psychological challenge, made particularly difficult by the fact that we have to combine our time preference with our feelings about risk itself as we contemplate the future consequences of the decisions we make today.

In my first book *What's Your Future Worth?*, I described how important it is for an individual to understand their own time preference and for each of us to know how much we value our long-term future compared to the value we place on our current situation. In *Thinking in*

Bets, Annie described how important it is for individuals to understand how they feel about risk when they are about to make a decision that has both positive and negative potential outcomes. We need to do both, and we need to do them at the same time, because many important financial decisions include both significant risk and years between when the decision is made and when the consequences will be felt.

So how do we do this?

First, it is important to know what *not* to do. Fundamentally, both risk aversion (attraction?) and time preference are individual and subjective. As we have said throughout this book and as principle #1 explicitly states, every financial decision should be made consistent with who *you* are as a person, with your individual circumstances and individual values and attitudes. Therefore, first know that there is no "right" answer. That's not to say there aren't programming flaws in our brains that may cause us to misunderstand or misevaluate our true preferences. There are many, and we will talk about them at length in the next few chapters.

Now, however, I want to mention one more technique that Annie outlined in her book for exploring one's feelings about risk, that is, the "mental time travel." It is a thought experiment that anyone can perform when facing an important financial decision. While designed to address risk tolerance, she and I have discussed and agreed that it can also be effectively applied to help you determine your time preference. It can help you hone in on your own personal rate of discount, which will help you make better long-term financial decisions.

As Annie says, the key problem we face is that we "don't feel the consequences of most of the decisions we make right away." I would argue that to the extent we are successful at living in the moment, we are also blissfully unaware of how we will feel many years in the future when the full consequences of our long-term financial decisions regarding key issues like our retirement planning are fully manifest.

Fundamentally, mental time travel entails imagining, in a very concrete way, what your future self will be like. Annie describes this process in some depth and suggests that there are even some technology apps that can help you do this (e.g., Merrill Lynch's Face Retirement[101] app that lets you literally see what you will look like many years in the future).

For risk tolerance, the use of mental time travel is straightforward. You envision how you will feel if any number of the future outcomes come to pass, and then you decide just how much you want to avoid each of those risky alternatives.

Determining your time preference is a little different. You need to compare the way you will feel in *two imaginary futures* (e.g., the one where you ended up saving for retirement and the one where you didn't) and compare that difference to how you evaluate the difference between *two alternative presents* (the one where you spend the big bonus you got and the one where you put all of it into your 401(k) account). It is the relative value of those four versions of yourself that will determine the time preference component of your personal discount rate.

Mental time travel is not easy, and it is not precise. For those interested in getting better at it, I suggest you pick up *Thinking in Bets* where Annie devotes an entire chapter to it. But now let's move on to what is perhaps the most frustrating of all the challenges we face when we try to manage our financial lives—understanding ourselves, including the irrational and often unconscious biases that millions of years of human evolution have left us with.

SECTION IV

Knowing Yourself—It's
an Irrational World

Chapter 10
What We Thought We Knew Was Wrong

The mid-1980s was a heady time for investment professionals. The truly scary inflation and interest rates of the late seventies and early eighties had abated somewhat (ten-year treasuries peaked in September 1981 at the currently inconceivable level of 15.76 percent)[102] and were now within hailing distance of historical norms. The stock market and the economy were roaring (the Crash of 1987 was still a couple years in the future), and it seemed that with the accelerating advances in both computer technology and investment theory, the world was on the brink of a new era where the mysteries of risk and return would finally be unraveled, and we could all look forward to a bright and secure financial future.

I had just become an Associate in the Society of Actuaries (ASA) and was starting to take my Fellowship exams, an important one of which was on Economics, which specifically addressed the investment of the billions (now trillions) of dollars set aside to pay for the liabilities that we as actuaries are charged with managing. It was with some eager curiosity that I sat down in the spring of 1986 to begin studying modern portfolio theory, developed by Harry Markowitz,[103] the first of several dense books and papers that comprised the almost 1,200 pages of the exam syllabus.

Sadly, my enthusiasm lasted less than a page. In the second paragraph of the opening chapter, I read the stunningly blithe statement, "People are risk averse." Based on that "fact," the remainder of the book would lay out for the reader a beautiful and powerful theory of the "efficient frontier" that purported to demonstrate how, for different levels of risk tolerance, a mix of investments could be developed to maximize expected returns, thus allowing one to be maximally "efficient" in one's investment strategy. This was "state of the art" and therefore it was incumbent on me as an actuary to be well aware of how the investment professionals charged with managing the asset side of the equation were doing their job.

At the time, I had only been in the business world for a little less than seven years, but even in that short time, I had learned enough practical risk management to know that the statement above was worse than wrong—it was meaningless. To think that the entire edifice of investment theory (as well as the financial security of millions of policyholders and pension plan participants) was built on such a shaky foundation was a truly frightening thought. As I stared again and again at those four words, I seriously considered abandoning my goal of becoming a fully credentialed actuary and resigning myself to a career as a technical practitioner (the only path then available to a career ASA).

To understand how misguided the statement about people's risk aversion was, it is important to first realize that people are not uniformly risk averse. Daniel Kahneman and Amos Tversky[104] would demonstrate this definitively in a few years, but even then, there were anomalous behaviors that were already obvious to anyone who looked that made those of us in the business doubt the conventional wisdom regarding risk aversion. But, even more importantly, people don't even know what risk is. Hell, I didn't even know what it was, and risk was the core concept of my whole profession.

As I said, in order to become an ASA, I had to learn all the relevant actuarial mathematics. While that entailed a fairly deep dive into probability and statistics, it also required passing a full actuarial exam devoted to risk theory itself. Risk theory, as taught to actuaries at the time, was a brutally difficult subject. Not only was the math barely penetrable, but the questions were very deep. If you thought too much about them, you would quickly find yourself mired in unanswerable philosophical questions about knowability. It could cause you to doubt the efficacy of even studying the subject.

With respect to the exam on risk theory, there was no choice. I put aside my existential angst, dug in to learn the math, and eventually passed the exam. Later, with a book on modern portfolio theory open in front of me, I faced the even more daunting task of suspending my disbelief to learn a theory whose fundamental assumption was clearly flawed. Nevertheless, I was pragmatic. I held my nose, read the material, and passed that exam as well, eventually going on to get my Fellowship.

Little did I realize it, but at almost the exact moment I was studying modern portfolio theory, Daniel Kahneman and Amos Tversky were in the process of inventing the field of behavioral economics. It is based on the proposition that we are NOT rational decision-makers. Our attitudes toward risk, reward, and economic decisions, in general, are far more complex and context-dependent than anyone had previously thought. Virtually all economic and investment theories, including Markowitz's, were fundamentally flawed.

Before we get to the specific discoveries of Kahneman, Tversky, and several others who destroyed, once and for all, the notion that we are rational when it comes to money, I want to follow my own journey just a little bit further. In addition to recognizing that we are not rational when it comes to risk, I quickly found that my clients and the employees that they represented were distinctly irrational when it came to one other key component of financial decision-making—incorporating the element of *time* into an evaluation of the trade-offs between costs and benefits in the future versus those in the present.

In my job, I observed countless pension plan participants making the "wrong" decision by electing a lump sum cash-out in lieu of a guaranteed lifetime pension when they reached retirement. I knew these decisions were objectively wrong because I was the one having to calculate the "lump sum equivalent option" to send to prospective retirees. The lump sums offered by companies to their employees were only equivalent if the retiree could manage to earn an extremely high investment return (sometimes double digit) *and* manage the systematic spending of the lump sum to last the rest of the retiree's (and sometimes his/her spouse's) life. To me, this was the height of irrationality, and it had very little to do with risk aversion. Instead, it had to do with time preference. While any actuary could tell you that people don't balance the present and the future in a logical way (taking into account reasonable investment returns), economists and financial experts had no good explanation for the phenomenon. Instead, they simply ignored it.

I actually formulated my own theory about it, calling it the "Time Value of Time" and got it published in one of the actuarial journals.[105] Unfortunately, readership was limited, and it never caught on. However, while I was telling everyone who would listen that pension plan participants shouldn't be allowed to damage themselves by being given choices that they were guaranteed to get wrong, Richard H. Thaler[106] was investigating the subject of time preference in a more systematic and comprehensive way. Along with Kahneman and Tversky, Thaler's work stands as one of the most important nails in the coffin of modern economic theory. In a minute, we will look at what Thaler discovered, but first, let's take a closer look at behavioral economics and how it came to be.

For those interested in how we came to understand that what we thought we knew was wrong, I suggest you read *The Undoing Project* by Michael Lewis.[107] Lewis is a terrific writer who has written some riveting books about how human foibles have led the world of money to the brink of catastrophe several times in just the last few decades. *The Big Short*[108,109] is probably the one most of you are familiar with, as it was made into a wonderfully coherent movie about the financial crisis of 2008–2009, but many of his other books are also well worth reading.

If you want to know his origin story as a financial war correspondent, you should check out *Liar's Poker,*"[110] which details how Lewis spent the early years of his career being a fly on the wall at Salomon Brothers in the 1980s. At the time, the technology arms race had begun in the investment banking world. An unconscionable amount of money was made by very smart people who thought little about the long-term consequences of their new investment products and strategies. Many of Lewis's subsequent books address little-known stories about hidden aspects of how investment professionals do (mostly legal) things that create peril for individuals venturing into the markets on their own. *Flash Boys*[111] is a good example. It describes the lightning speed trading that allows traders to shave pennies off both sides of their high frequency trades, leaving normal investors to buy at a higher price and sell at a lower one.

Lewis understands as well as I do how dangerous the Money Mountain wilderness is, even when you are able to act rationally. In *The Undoing Project*, he describes the discovery by the pioneers of behavioral economists that we are decidedly *not* rational. In fact, our internal wiring makes us vulnerable and unprepared as individuals to survive in this environment.

The Undoing Project follows the story of Kahneman and Tversky as they began to map the hitherto unknown regions of the human psyche where decisions are actually made. Through introspection, observation, and ingenious experiments, the two of them discovered that when faced with basic probability or financial questions (e.g., "What is the chance that in a group of one hundred people, two or more have the same birthday?" Or "Would you rather have a 10 percent chance of receiving $1,000 or a guaranteed fifty dollars?"), humans not only were inconsistent, often providing different answers when the same question is worded slightly differently, but even when the answers were consistent, they were often in direct conflict with both logic and what mainstream economic theory would predict.

Kahneman and Tversky were extraordinary collaborators as well as interesting people. They were each great thinkers in their own right. The world owes them a debt of gratitude for their discoveries of many of the most ubiquitous emotional biases and cognitive errors we are prone to. In the next chapter, we will go through an inventory of some of the most important ones that can trip you up as you try to make good financial decisions. Before we do that, I want to talk about Richard H. Thaler and his work on time preference as the way we balance and value what happens tomorrow vs. what we experience today, and the conclusions I've come to about how to use his stunning insights. As we have discussed previously, this is an absolutely critical component of almost every financial decision you will have to make.

As I said, in 1997, the magazine *Contingencies* published my own small contribution to the conversation.[112] In that article, I posited that perhaps because of the way we perceive the *flow* of time (i.e., that the years seem to go faster as we get older), we choose to value the present more highly than the future. In fact, that is why my pension clients persisted in taking their pensions as a lump sum rather than doing the rational thing and opting for a guaranteed life annuity. I was not in an academic setting, so I had no requirement for getting my work peer-reviewed, but I did send an advance copy to Andrew Abel who was a professor at Wharton and the best economist I knew.[113] Andy was kind enough to read my article and send me back a survey of all the current economic papers being done on the concept of time preference, which, in mainstream economic theory, was considered a relatively insignificant, though occasionally troubling, parameter that had to be incorporated into models of how investment markets and the economy in general operated.

It was a bit of an eye-opener to me to see that economists were looking at the same factor that I, as an actuary, was concerned about, albeit through a slightly different lens. I was, therefore, very curious to see whether the experts in the field had happened on the same phenomenon as I had.

In fact, almost none of them had—that is, except for Richard H. Thaler who was then an economics professor at Cornell University.[114] Thaler had written a paper in 1981 confirming that people use a "hyperbolic discount rate" to choose between costs and benefits provided now vs. alternatives available in the future. This was precisely the phenomenon I was writing about and explained why so many of my clients took lump sum distributions rather than the more rational choice of a lifetime annuity. Even though his paper had been written more than a decade before my magazine article, it seemed that the world still did not appreciate the significance of Thaler's work. The material that Andy had sent me showed clearly that even though time preference was not well-understood by economists, none of the anomalies that Thaler identified were affecting the conventional wisdom as to how either economic or actuarial work should be done.

Thaler did finally get the accolades and credit for his groundbreaking insights into how and why mainstream economic theory was wrong, eventually winning the Nobel Prize[115] for his brilliant work. He did much more than discover hyperbolic discounting. He also identified the endowment effect[116] and many other biases and cognitive quirks that make our economic lives difficult. In the next chapter, we will go through the most important of them and talk about what you can do to prevent them from sabotaging your financial situation. At this time, let's continue with why I believe that this particular quirk of our brains is more a feature of who we are rather than a psychological defect that we should attempt to compensate or rely on experts to help us overcome.

Of all of Thaler's discoveries, hyperbolic discounting is probably the one that he is most famous for, mostly because of the way it has been illustrated and addressed in our world today. In particular, many have taken Thaler's work to be evidence of our inclination to be unreasonably impatient and to instinctually choose immediate gratification instead of prudently and appropriately sacrificing immediate gain for much greater rewards in the future.

Many of you have probably watched the adorable YouTube video of five-year-olds taking the marshmallow test[117] that theoretically can be used to predict future success in the world based on whether an individual has the innate capability to plan for the future and defer immediate gratification to achieve more in the long run. In that test, a young child is given a marshmallow and told that they can eat it now or wait ten minutes, in which case the grown-up will come back and give them a second marshmallow. The key is that if the child doesn't wait and instead eats the marshmallow in front of him before the researcher returns, they will forfeit the opportunity to get a second treat. I don't know whether or not passing the test is predictive of anything, but the video does make for a compelling demonstration of our idiosyncratic differences in how we value the now vs. the later.

Thaler himself has advocated for applying his principles to making changes in the way our society is run that will help people overcome their impatience and reduce suffering. His book *Nudge*[118] describes many of these changes, which, I believe, are good, particularly those that retain our ability to override the system and still grab that marshmallow in front of us. For example, many companies now use a negative election approach to enrollment in their 401(k) plans. Under a negative election, unless they explicitly opt out, employees are enrolled in the plan as soon as they are eligible, and a percent of their paycheck is automatically deducted and deposited into their account. This has undoubtedly increased 401(k) participation nationwide and likely increased, at least somewhat, the retirement security that many employees will have down the road. The fact that it is optional and that employees can still decide not to participate and/or save a smaller percentage of their income provides, in my opinion, the best of both worlds. It is when these nudges become mandatory or when experts put undue pressure on people to accept their nudges that I become concerned.

The argument for those who would believe in protecting us from ourselves goes as follows. Over the millennia, our biological evolution has produced within us what seem like "programming bugs." Many of these bugs served us well when we roamed the savannah and needed to eat or avoid being eaten by saber-toothed tigers, but they do not serve us so well in the modern world. Undoubtedly, this is true when it comes to our difficulties in evaluating the likelihood of various future scenarios; both on an individual basis (e.g., our risk of getting in an accident, suffering imminent death, disability, or loss of job), and on a more macro-economic basis (e.g., the likelihood of a stock market crash, changes in inflation/interest rates). Those who take issue with personal rates of discount also argue that we are programmed to overvalue the present, perhaps because primitive man's future was so fraught with risk and danger. Therefore, a key role of actuaries and other financial planners is to deprogram individuals with our expertise and therefore enable them to make better decisions that will lead to better outcomes and less regret.

My primary objection to this is that I see a fundamental difference between the objective evaluation of real-world risks (like the probability that the plane you are on will crash or that you will have a heart attack and die the next year) and a determination of what is basically an internal set of feelings about the way you live your life. I think it is highly presumptuous for anyone to tell me what I will or will not regret thirty years from now. How many stories have we all heard of people at the end of their life regretting all the rational financial decisions they have made instead of taking that trip around the world, spending more time with loved ones, and generally experiencing life in the moment? It's not an easy thing, but I don't think such tradeoffs between the now and the later should *ever* be outsourced.

Beyond this, I believe there are objective reasons why expert opinion on discount rates is often wrong and less reliable than what an individual—who has taken the time to educate themselves on the technical considerations of the financial decision to be made—can do with access to information about their own desires and values that an expert can never know. For those interested in that aspect of why I believe everyone should develop their own personal discount rate, you can read an essay I wrote on the subject ("In Defense of Personal Rates of Discount"),[119] which is still available on my website.

Now let us turn to the broader issue of how we can become aware and manage the myriad other ways in which our brains irrationally process information and evaluate the choices we face each day.

Chapter 11
Biases, Heuristics, and Cognitive Errors

I dedicated my first book to my friend Robert Frohlich, a childhood friend who died shortly before I began writing *What's Your Future Worth?* Rob always told me that he knew nothing about money. In fact, whenever I asked him how he was doing, he would say that everything was going great, mostly because he was doing exactly what he wanted in the world and the only (small) problem he had was that he was broke. To him, not having enough money was only a minor inconvenience, and given the way he lived his life, it made a world of sense.

Rob was a freelance ski journalist who lived in the Sierra Mountains near Lake Tahoe. He may not have made enough with his writing to pay his rent on time, but he had a season pass to every ski resort in the area. He was welcomed at pretty much any other ski mountain in the US he chose to visit, as well as many resorts in Europe as well. His list of friends included professional ski racers, mountain explorers, and extreme skiers of all types. He was well-loved everywhere he went. After he passed away in 2010, over a thousand people, including many famous adventurers and former Olympians, filled one of the hotel auditoriums in Squaw Valley to honor his life. In short, he died a wealthy man—not in terms of money, but in terms of the rich relationships he built and the legacy he left behind.

Not surprisingly, Rob was an extraordinary skier. In many ways, he viewed his life as one long downhill run on a double black diamond trail—full of moguls, rocks, trees, uneven snow with icy patches, and weather conditions that could change in an instant. When I watched him make his way down an impossibly steep pitch, he looked completely calm, relaxed, and in control, not of the environment he was navigating, but of himself. His body, boots, skis, and poles all seemed to be natural extensions of his limbs. He recognized and exemplified the fact that skiing down a mountain requires complete awareness of your surroundings along with all the ways your body might fall prey to the hazards of the environment. Rob always knew where he was going, but his attention was on the present, making sure his next turn was crisp, precise, and true to the route down the mountain that he had chosen.

In the first ten chapters of this book, we have discussed the terrain of the world of money, and now we need to take a closer look at ourselves and the limitations we have when we go money mountaineering. Just like Rob, who had a deep understanding of all the ways his body and mind could cause him to crash and fall, we need to understand where our weaknesses in making financial decisions lie, where we can get fooled into thinking the path is clearer and the trail is wider and emptier than it really is.

Since Kahneman, Tversky, Thaler, and a few others have invented behavioral economics, the field has exploded with hundreds of books written on the subject. With all that new knowledge, we can now consider the full range of our brains' programming bugs that have been identified, along with an equal number of suggested fixes.

In the next chapter, we will talk again with Annie Duke and look at her tips for surviving in the wilderness. For now, however, it would be useful to simply identify among those human idiosyncrasies which are the ones we need to be most attentive to when faced with financial choices.

By now, our knowledge of the number of emotional biases and systematic cognitive errors that we are prone to has grown tremendously. The line between what is an emotional bias or a cognitive error is often a fine one. With so many of these phenomena interrelated, it is hard to keep track of them all, let alone know which ones are the most important to look out for. The proliferation of all the various ways in which humans differ from the "homo-economicus" that mainstream economic theory has historically assumed has made it challenging for the academic world to find a better model. Clearly, the old one is broken, but no comprehensive and compelling economic theory has yet been developed to replace it.

Fortunately, you don't need to worry about understanding how the world of money really works. As we discussed at the very beginning, as overwhelmingly complex and incomprehensible as the system is, all you need to understand is *your* system. While complex, it is much less so than the one we are embedded in, and it is a system that *you* can be an expert on. For those who like to get the full story, in the end notes of this book, you will find what Wikipedia considers a complete inventory of emotional biases and cognitive errors.[120]

While I encourage you to take a look at what Wikipedia has done, I have laid out below a summary of what I consider the most important biases and errors you should be aware of as you embark on your quest for financial wellness. Again, this summary is by no means complete, and I may have even left out some important ones. After all, I am prone to the same biases as everyone else, so my curation is far from objective. Nevertheless, I believe it is a useful start.

Emotional Biases

1. *Endowment Effect* – This was Thaler's first discovery, and it is vitally important to consider whether you are prone to it. Being under its influence can lead to serious financial mistakes. Essentially, the endowment effect causes you to overvalue what you already have and undervalue what you haven't yet acquired. It can cause you, for example, to hold on to investments you should sell and not invest in assets that you should be investing in.
2. *Confirmation Bias* – This tendency to seek confirmation of what you already believe can cause you to ignore relevant data, accept confirmatory data without due diligence, or rely too much on

experts whose conclusions fit your pre-existing beliefs. It was first discovered by psychologists in the 1960s, but its prevalence and impact on people's behavior was only more fully explored as the field of behavioral economics evolved.

3. *Hindsight/Outcome Bias* – Annie Duke addresses this in the first chapter of *Thinking in Bets*, and it is a source of unnecessary suffering for all of us. Annie calls it "resulting," which means we confuse the quality of the decisions we make with how they turn out. It causes us to regret good decisions that turned out badly. Even worse, it drives us to make future bad decisions because we rely on what has been successful for us in the past, not thinking clearly about the decision at hand. Annie is an expert at overcoming this bias, and I would recommend again reading both *Thinking in Bets* and her latest book, *How to Decide*,[121] to get better at avoiding this bias.

4. *Availability Bias* – The identification of this bias and the exploration of the variety of ways it can manifest was, in my view, one of Kahneman and Tversky's greatest achievements. It means relying most on what we remember best (i.e., experiences that are "available" to us) when deciding what to do next. If, for example, you lost your house in the financial crisis of 2008–2009, you might have an unrealistic estimate of how likely a similar real estate crash is to happen again in the next few years. It's not that you would be wrong to be concerned that another crash might happen, but availability bias could easily distort your estimate of exactly what the probability of it happening is and what steps you should take regarding your real estate investments.

5. *Anchoring Bias* – This bias is a close cousin to availability bias. It turns out that we don't need to have been traumatized by a real estate crash to distort our view of what will happen next. All we need is to be primed with an initial prompt. Kahneman and Tversky elegantly demonstrated the existence of the anchoring bias[122] by showing that, when given the challenge of quickly calculating 8 x 7 x 6 x 5 x 4 x 3 x 2 x 1, they got a bigger number than when they were asked to calculate the other way around,

that is, 1 x 2 x 3 x 4 x 5 x 6 x 7 x 8. That is the essence of the anchoring bias and it can wreak havoc with your evaluation of different investments if you are not careful.

6. *Loss/Dread Aversion* – It has been known for many years that people suffer more when they lose $1,000 than feel happy when they win it. I'm speculating, but this phenomenon may, to some degree, be why the notion that the statement "People are risk averse" seemed like such a reasonable assumption to those who developed modern portfolio theory. In fact, we seem to act as if losses are about twice as impactful as gains. Of course, it is more complicated than that (which is one of the reasons Markowitz was wrong). When the endowment effect is considered at the same time, the situation becomes even more complex. It is also not just losses that we recoil from, it is the *possibility* of it (i.e., dread) that we also avoid to an irrational extent.

7. *Normalcy/Conservatism Bias* – This is a relatively recently discovered bias that occurs in about 70 percent of us, while much of the other 30 percent are prone to "overreaction bias." In some ways, this is less an emotional bias than an inability of humans to quickly and accurately assess whether what might happen is governed by one of the fat-tailed distributions we have discussed periodically throughout this book. Most of us *want* to believe that randomness follows a normal distribution. Unfortunately, it often doesn't, and while our brains may have evolved to protect us from the extreme dangers we have historically faced, I don't believe they are well suited to the kind of financial catastrophes that can occur today.

8. *The Dunning–Kruger Effect*[123] – This is an effect that was first identified in 1999 by the second-generation behavioral economists David Dunning and Justin Kruger. They studied how people consistently overestimated their skill in domains for which they had not been trained. This is very important when it comes to financial matters, as overconfidence in one's abilities can be dangerous. This is in no way inconsistent with the basic premise of this book, which suggests that individuals need to take

ownership of their own financial choices. It just means that you
need to assume that you know less than you think you know.

The distinction between emotional biases and systematic cognitive
errors is, in some sense, an arbitrary one. We often make cognitive errors
because of our emotional biases, but I do believe it is useful to identify
some of the common ways that we systematically make logical or calcu-
lation mistakes when we try to evaluate financial choices even after we
have made sure that we are not suffering from any of the biases/effects
listed above.

Systematic Cognitive Errors

1. *Misunderstanding of Probability and Statistics* – This is a very
   broad category and fundamentally stems from the fact that our
   brains just aren't wired to do sophisticated math on the fly. It is
   especially true when we are facing important financial choices
   and have neither the training nor the time to do a full calcu-
   lation. A full enumeration of all the mistakes we make here is
   beyond the scope of this book, but in the next chapter, we will
   discuss, with advice from Annie Duke, how best to overcome
   this inherent handicap in our makeup.
2. *The Money Illusion*[124] – The money illusion was identified by
   Tversky in some of the work he did on his own after his collaboration with Kahneman ended. Tversky found that when evaluating money, people will focus on its nominal value rather than
   the purchasing power of the sum involved. This is particularly
   important when the financial choice involves a long period of
   time during which inflation may erode the purchasing power of
   the proceeds realizable from the sale of a particular investment.
3. *Ignoring Survivorship Effects* – This effect is most apparent when
   people evaluate the historical performance of a particular investment manager relative to a benchmark or the average of all
   managers over a given period. By just looking at the historical

record of a particular manager, people often do not take into account that the manager in question is still in business and that the benchmark or average might include those that are already out of the business. We addressed this phenomenon in Section II when we discussed the sales techniques used by investment managers to convince investors of their superior performance.

4. *Other Logical Fallacies* – In addition to making basic mistakes in calculating probabilities, our brains have developed a number of heuristics (i.e., shortcuts) that often lead us astray. No one that I know has put them into a coherent hierarchy, but a few of the most important ones (for financial purposes) are described here.

The first is the *gambler's fallacy*. This is our tendency to think that if you flip a coin five times and it comes up heads each time, then it is more likely than not that the sixth flip will come up tails because the coin is due. The best recipe for this is to keep telling yourself that the dice, or coins, have no memory.

Another important one related to the gambler's fallacy is the *hot hand fallacy*. This is our tendency to believe that streaks, particularly the ones that we experience (either lucky or unlucky), are due to something other than randomness. Sometimes they are, but all too often, we reject randomness as an explanation and ascribe control or some other unseen force to what we are observing. This is a particularly dangerous phenomenon when you are tempted to invest in a business that appears to be on a winning streak for which you don't have a good explanation.

Another more subtle error that people make is the *base rate fallacy*, which can lead you to think that you have found an investment opportunity when all you are looking at is a "noisy line of transmission." The best example of this is to consider how the rate of false positives can lead you to overestimate the likelihood of the phenomenon you are observing. Consider a breathalyzer test that is 95 percent accurate. Out of every one hundred sober drivers tested, only five are shown to be drunk even though they aren't. If only one of the hundred drivers on the road is actually drunk, then if all of them are tested and you fail your breathalyzer test, it is highly likely that you have been falsely accused, being one of the four or five false positives rather than the one driver who was actually drunk.

Finally, there is the *conjunction fallacy,* which was one of Kahneman and Tversky's most famous discoveries.[125] We often make this error when we feel that the conjunction of two characteristics is more likely than the likelihood of just one of the two characteristics. This is particularly true when the two characteristics seem to be highly correlated. Kahneman and Tversky describe it best:

"Linda is thirty-one years old, single, outspoken, and very bright. She majored in philosophy. As a student, she was deeply concerned with issues of discrimination and social justice, and also participated in anti-nuclear demonstrations.

Which is more probable?

Linda is a bank teller.

Linda is a bank teller and is active in the feminist movement."

Clearly, the answer is that Linda is a bank teller, despite our feeling that she is much more than that. Sophisticated investment opportunities can be marketed in a way that takes advantage of this flaw in our brains, so one must be vigilant about this one.

Many of my friends and colleagues in the business world are not skiers but instead spend their leisure time playing golf. I have one friend in the investment world who believes that the same discipline and mindset that makes one a good golfer can be applied to one's financial world as well. He agrees that all of what I've laid out is true. He said that the attention one brings to correcting one's stance, grip, and swing is the same kind of self-awareness that can be brought to bear when facing an important financial decision and needing to make sure that one's emotional biases are put aside and cognitive errors are guarded against. Maybe so, but for me, Rob's approach to downhill skiing resonates more deeply.

In golf, the ball sits silent and still as you take your time to examine your lie and where you want your shot to land. You consider your options and choose the right club. Only then do you align yourself, adjust your stance, steady your mind, and begin your swing. You know that once you hit the ball, you have very few random variables to worry about, really only the wind and the bounce that the ball takes after it lands.

When you are skiing, just like in life, the decisions come fast and furiously, the terrain is continuously changing, and what you will be facing a few turns down the unseen slope is often completely unknown.

My advice to you then as you set out on your financial path is to do what Rob told me to do when he took me down my first expert run thirty years ago—keep your knees bent, your head up, and lean over your skis. Be ready for the unexpected and know that the only thing you can really control is yourself. You do your best to make the right choices and avoid trouble when you see it, and then just accept what comes next. Sometimes it is an easy wide slope you can cruise down, but sometimes it's another sharp turn you have to make, and often, it can be sooner than you expected.

Chapter 12
Making Better Bets—
Overcoming Our Limitations

Pre COVID-19, I struggled with what felt like one of the most important decisions I'd ever faced. It was not financial, but rather a medical one with impossibly high stakes. Since the pandemic hit us, I and perhaps many of you have faced even scarier choices, but for me, this was the first decision I had ever faced where the stakes were literally life or death.

Like many medical decisions, it was a bet with a limited upside, but one with a downside that ranged from very bad to catastrophic. It may not be an all-in bet like the ones we talked about in Chapter 9, but it was pretty close.

My annual physical included a blood test that indicated a potential problem, which could have been any number of things. There was also a material chance that it was cancer. If it was, further tests were needed to determine whether it was a slow-growing form that would not require immediate treatment or if it was aggressive. If it was the latter, I would then need to quickly undergo radiation and/or surgery to avoid dying. The next step recommended by my doctor was to get a biopsy that would determine both whether I had cancer and, if so, what form it was.

This was pretty shocking news to me, made even more frightening when it was explained that because the growth was in a hard-to-reach spot, the biopsy itself was going to be an invasive procedure with significant risks. In other words, I needed more data to make a decision entailing a high stakes risk/reward tradeoff. However, even getting that additional data would entail balancing the value of the information with the risk of damaging my body in the attempt to get that information.

For several reasons, the choice was more complicated than that. For one thing, I wasn't sure how reliable the results of the blood test were. Medical tests of all kinds (including biopsies) are not 100 percent accurate, sometimes giving false positives or false negatives. In this case, the doctors told me that while my blood test was generally very reliable, biopsies can produce up to 20 percent false negatives, in which case, a second biopsy might have to be done if I wanted to be really sure that the result I had gotten was accurate.

With respect to the numbers themselves, my blood test results suggested I had a 30 percent probability of having cancer, but even that number seemed potentially subject to selection bias; that is, 30 percent of those who have had a biopsy were found to have cancer, ignoring the unknown number of those with similar test results who chose NOT to have a biopsy. Nevertheless, it was the best estimate I had for my chance of having the dreaded disease.

What really concerned me, however, was that the biopsy itself was a dangerous and uncertain proposition. As noted above, the literature suggested that there was a 20 percent chance of a false negative result for a biopsy (i.e., that even though I had cancer, the biopsy result would say I didn't). Second, this kind of biopsy is very invasive. The studies I looked at suggested that there was an 8 percent to 10 percent chance of unpleasant side effects, the most serious of which is 3 percent to 4 percent chance of getting an antibiotic-resistant infection that could put me in the hospital. To me, that was a serious risk indeed, as my wife had previously suffered a similar infection that had put her in the hospital for six days and almost killed her. This scared me, and even though I knew I might be overreacting due to availability bias, I couldn't help but worry about that possibility.

Even though all the doctors I spoke to uniformly recommended that I get the biopsy, I wasn't convinced. The way I looked at it, all I would get from the biopsy was *information*. That information might very well be critical to making my next decision (i.e., whether and what treatment to undergo), but in and of itself, the biopsy would only reduce the uncertainty I had about my health. If I did have it, it *might* provide me with more control over it in the future. I needed to consider how valuable that information was and what I was willing to pay to get it.

It seemed to me that the important upside of a biopsy was finding out early that I had a fast-growing cancer that would kill me if I didn't fix it. Apparently, with new treatments, they could get rid of such cancers with almost 100 percent effectiveness. Getting an estimate of *that* probability was an extremely difficult task. It was, however, easy to estimate the downside risk of getting the biopsy—a one in twenty-five chance that I would end up in the hospital with a life-threatening infection.

Making things even more complicated, there appeared to be some promising new diagnostic alternatives (e.g., detailed MRI scans) that would soon be able to get the same information without the same risks that my biopsy would entail. I had to consider how long I could wait to take advantage of those new diagnostic tools. If I did have cancer and it was slow growing, I would have plenty of time. If it was aggressive, there simply was no telling, and there was no data to help me with that question.

Finally, I had to consider one last factor that we have talked about previously—my personal discount rate. If I had the biopsy and ended up in the hospital, that would be an *immediate* cost. Not having the biopsy could lead to costs—that is, having to treat either a slow- or fast-growing cancer—that would not take place until sometime in the future, potentially years hence if the cancer was slow growing. Of course, in the seven out of ten chances that I didn't have cancer, I wouldn't have any cost at all. The long-term benefit of knowing that *this* hazard was off the table would simply be the comfort of knowing that I could get on with my life with one less thing to worry about.

This last factor caused me to also consider what would happen if I delayed my biopsy. When I asked the question, my doctor informed me that if I waited, and I had a problem, my blood tests would likely get worse; if not, they would probably stay the same or even get better. When I heard that news, I realized I was looking at what was almost, in Annie Duke's language, a "free roll," where doing nothing would give me more information and avoid, at least for the moment, the necessity of taking on a risk that had a substantial downside. Based on this last bit of data, I decided to defer the biopsy for a few months and then see what a follow-up blood test showed.

I felt pretty good about my analysis. Before I read *Thinking in Bets*, I probably would have stopped there and proceeded with my intended plan without any qualms. But something continued to nag at the edge of my conscious brain.

I asked myself "What would Annie do?" particularly since, as I thought again about my decision to defer the biopsy, I wondered whether I was falling prey to one or more of the many emotional biases and systematic cognitive errors that are serious challenges to all of us when facing difficult decisions under uncertainty.

It turns out that Annie had a lot to say that was useful.

In Chapter 9, we discussed Annie's advice on what kind of attitude one needs to thrive in an uncertain and unpredictable world. Now we will talk about some of the practical techniques she has developed to help individuals overcome the emotional biases and cognitive system bugs we all have.

Much of my hesitation to get a biopsy stemmed from my fear that I would end up just like my wife a few years earlier—in the hospital with a life-threatening infection. While I concluded that that was a significant risk on the order of 1/25, in rereading *Thinking in Bets*, I realized that my determination of that number could easily have been affected by availability bias. This bias causes us to overestimate the probability of events that are similar to ones we have experienced ourselves, and so I took another look at why I came to the conclusion I did.

My 4 percent estimate was based on a review of some studies that addressed this very issue, but what I didn't do was talk to other experts in the field to get their view of those same studies. I had unfairly assumed that most doctors were going to be biased and underplay the risks because "to a man with a hammer, everything looks like a nail."

In fact, I still believe that my concern about doctors' bias is not only well-founded, but is made worse by *confirmation bias* that arises because so much of what passes as expert opinion comes from knowledgeable people with the same orientation speaking to each other and not getting a diversity of perspectives. We discussed this problem as well earlier. Now it is time to talk about the solution.

So how can one guard against one's own emotional biases like availability bias while getting good information that is free of confirmation bias?

One of Annie's solutions is to use a buddy system. In Chapter 4[126] of *Thinking in Bets*, she describes this technique in detail. Fundamentally, using a buddy system means accessing a group of friendly experts to help you make important decisions. There are many aspects to the buddy system that are not always practical (e.g., experts should be accountable for the consequences of their advice), but much of her recommendations were directly applicable to my biopsy decision and can be used effectively for financial decisions as well.

Perhaps the most important characteristic of the group to which you are turning for advice is that the group includes a diversity of perspectives. As Annie says, "Diversity and dissent are not only checks on fallibility, but the only means of testing the truth of an opinion."[127] When too many like-minded experts are asked about an issue, the answers tend to be not only the same (which limits the range of alternatives you might consider), but also can be subject to "groupthink" and confirmatory thinking. Remember that confirmation bias is one of the most dangerous systematic cognitive errors we tend to make when facing a question. In other words, if I let another doctor know that I've already received a recommendation from my oncologist to get the biopsy, that doctor may be more inclined to agree with the one who has examined me and say that I should get the procedure.

A diversity of perspective does more. As Annie goes on to say, when we "get exposed to diverse opinions, (we) can test alternative hypotheses and move toward accuracy."[128] In my case, I asked not just other medical doctors I knew, but also my acupuncturist/herbalist (an expert in Chinese medicine), my therapist (a Ph.D. in psychology), and some of my actuarial/statistician friends who knew a bit about the validity and reliability of the tests that were producing the probabilities I was evaluating.

For me, using the buddy system was extremely valuable. While my MD friends, not surprisingly, all encouraged me to get the biopsy, my therapist encouraged me to imagine how I might *feel* if one or more of the scenarios I envisioned came to pass. The statisticians highlighted where some of the studies I read confused correlation and causation, and my Chinese medicine expert apprised me of an herbal treatment that might directly arrest the growth of any cancer I might have. By consulting a variety of experts who each had different perspectives on the management of physical wellbeing, I was able to get a more complete picture of my decision and, at last, overcome my own inherent biases and cognitive limitations.

In the end, I chose to undergo the herbal treatment that my acupuncturist recommended for a few months and then had my blood tested again. When the new blood test showed no material improvement, I got a biopsy. I was immensely relieved to go through the procedure safely and get a negative test result to boot. With the clarity of mind given to me by my therapist around dealing with an uncertain future, I chose not to get a second biopsy to guard against the possibility of a false negative.

I have never felt healthier, and I believe that the buddy system helped me get to the right answer. However, I do know that I still might have a bad outcome if the biopsy did indeed give a false negative. In that event, I will do my best to have faith. I will avoid hindsight bias in my decision-making process and not commit the cardinal sin of "resulting" that is described at the very beginning of *Thinking in Bets*, where I might regret my decision just because it ended badly.

Applying the Buddy System to Financial Decisions

The buddy system can also work well when you are facing choices that could affect your financial health. In Chapter 6, we talked about finding truth seekers. In an ideal world, we could all consult a group of experts every time we faced an important financial choice, but for most of us, that is not a practical answer. Among other things, to get actual advice on a particular financial issue, you might have to pay for access to the necessary expertise, and then you will have to face the challenge of principle #3 and make sure the expert you are talking to does not have a hidden agenda. Also, since the buddy system entails gathering perspectives that may conflict with each other, you could end up feeling like you paid for advice that was "wrong."

It is better to cultivate relationships with friends whom you trust and respect, as well as work in a finance-related field, but who might not be an expert in financial wellness or even the particular issue you are dealing with.

Let's say, for example, you are just getting established professionally and you either have or are planning on starting a family. You decide that you would like to buy a house, but you are not sure where and what kind to buy. This could be one of the most important financial decisions in your life, and it is a very complicated one.

In addition to basic logistical considerations like what kind of neighborhood you want to live in, how close you want to be to your workplace(s), shops, and service providers (e.g., schools, hospitals, playgrounds, parks), you will have a vast array of purely financial issues to consider.

Like Yaron and Sarah whom we met earlier, you might have to balance the price of the house vs. the quality of the school system. You will almost certainly need to decide how much leverage (i.e., how big a mortgage) to add to your personal balance sheet. Even more importantly, you will have to assess both the local market in terms of the possible future appreciation/depreciation and your evaluation of the attractiveness of real estate as an asset class you want to invest in.

No single financial planner, no matter how well-informed, will be able to advise you on all of these issues. It is also unlikely that you will have enough time to seek out and vet multiple written sources on each relevant aspect. However, it may be that you will know different people who will be very knowledgeable on one or more of those issues (e.g., teachers, real estate professionals, friends who work in the banking or investment world). Use the principles of the buddy system to select a group of friends/advisors who can be sources of accurate, trustworthy, and *diverse* views. Make sure you get their opinions so that you can become aware of the biases you might have and guard against them. By collecting potential alternative perspectives from your buddies on the questions you ask, you will become better able to clearly see the decisions you face and all the ways your heart and mind can cloud your vision.

Much of *Thinking in Bets* and *How to Decide* are focused on developing the self-awareness of the biases that so often lead us astray. These books will help you hone your basic decision-making processes, and if you want to make smarter bets in your financial life, Annie Duke's techniques work every bit as well in the world of money as they do in other aspects of life.

SECTION V

Living in the Wilderness—How to Stay Financially Healthy

Chapter 13

Using the Six Principles of Holistic Financial Wellness

In order to climb the highest peaks in the financial wilderness, you have to have good shoes, the right attitude, and a strong back to carry all the equipment you will need. The air is thin, the footing can be treacherous, and the consequences of a misstep can be severe. Not everybody has the skill and risk tolerance for mountain climbing. Some get altitude sickness and many lack the strength or willingness to carry such a heavy backpack. Personally, I stick to where the footing is sure, and I don't carry too much with me. I choose trails where I am confident that I won't get lost but where there is an opportunity to get above the tree line and enjoy the view. While I avoid danger and am careful when exploring unfamiliar terrain, I also love to be outside wandering about and looking at the scenery.

But that's just me. Because I am not a technical climber, I can't tell you what kind of rope to bring or whether it's necessary to bring one in the first place. In the same way, I am not going to give you advice on how to use the complex but powerful financial instruments that are increasingly available (and sometimes effective) for individual investors of moderate means who want to make a lot of money. Instead, I will tell you about a few relatively straightforward tools that I know well and have used myself. Almost anyone can understand and use what I am about to describe. But first, we need to talk about what you need to help you determine your destination and plan your route.

PETER NEUWIRTH, FSA, FCA

I am not a financial planner, but I do occasionally help my friends look at their financial situation and develop their financial strategy. A few months ago, my friend Bob asked me to assess, from a holistic view, where he was financially and then, based on his goals, fears, hopes, and needs, help him figure out what, if anything, he needed to do differently from what he was doing now to ensure his long-term financial well-being.

Bob is an unusual guy. He is curious, fearless, savvy, and creative, but he is not a long-term thinker. After over twenty years of riding a fast elevator to one of the top floors in the Corporate Tower (in his case, the pharmaceutical wing), Bob found himself working as a highly-paid executive in a Fortune 50 company. Instead of settling for where he was or trying to get to the C-Suite, just a few floors higher, Bob decided to walk away from his job and become an author and entrepreneur. At the time, he was in his mid-forties, had two mortgages, three kids in private school, and a complicated personal life that included a large extended family in the US and overseas and interests that have him traveling extensively. Needless to say, the timing of his decision was surprising, but Bob does what his intuition and experience tell him. He doesn't do any detailed scenario building. He also doesn't always look at the entire picture, at least when it comes to what he does with his money (and his ability to earn it). His approach is to survey his immediate surroundings and make choices one by one, trusting that he will make more good choices than bad ones.

When I first looked at Bob's personal balance sheet, I was taken aback at the incredible variety of money-related ventures and investments he was involved in. At first glance, how he earned his money and where he put it looked extremely chaotic and uncoordinated. I was afraid that when I looked closely, I would find ticking time bombs with the potential to wreak havoc in his financial life.

Bob had plenty of investments I would never consider for myself, like above-market loans to family members (though, of course, it was just such a loan from my college girlfriend that allowed me to buy my first condo), but there were also lots of other "flyers" that he had taken that looked interesting, including several separate $10,000 bets on business ideas of some of his bright and creative friends.

The more I looked, the more convinced I became that Bob was employing exactly the kind of barbell strategy that I described in Chapter 8. His significant guaranteed pensions from his corporate years, along with royalties from his bestselling books, would provide him a safe and secure income he could live on if all else failed. In fact, that barbell was set up in almost an ideal way since, just when the royalty stream peters out (almost every bestseller eventually runs out of steam), he will have reached retirement age when his guaranteed pensions will go into payment status.

His other barbell, the one with unlimited upside potential, was also well-constructed. As we discussed in Chapter 8, when you are trying to take advantage of a fat-tailed distribution, the important thing is to have many small bets, and while you can expect to lose almost every single one of them, the one or two long shots that come in are likely to make you enough money to cover all your losses and then some.

I have provided this kind of consulting to dozens and dozens of friends, colleagues, and paying clients. Bob was the first client I have had for which I had no material suggested improvements in his strategy. He could tell you better than me, but if I were to venture a guess, I would say that the only value I was able to provide him was confirmation that he was on his way to financial wellness and that he should continue to maintain his clear-eyed and fearless attitude toward making his way up the peaks he was attempting to climb.

Bob found his strategy by intuition, and what I did was give him some analysis and theoretical grounding to validate what he was already doing. All he really needed was a bit of guidance about how all the pieces of his complicated financial life were related and a sense of what the future *might* look like if he continued on his path. Essentially, I provided him a pair of binoculars to scan the horizon and see if any potential hazards might throw him off the path he was on.

Before we move on to a discussion of the specific tools you should have in your backpack, I want to note one more aspect of why Bob is a true money mountaineer. Beyond his ability to focus on what is in front of him without worrying about an unpredictable future, Bob also manifests two behaviors that are important corollaries of the six HFW principles that we have been discussing throughout this book.

The first is that he believes that you should invest in what you know. This is wise advice that I first heard from Paul McCartney who, legend has it, became a very wealthy man not because of all the money he earned with the Beatles, but rather by the royalties he earned from owning the rights to his songs as well as those of other artists' songs that he had invested in along the way. Paul knew a good song when he heard one, and his judgment on which ones would provide an outsized return on investment has proven extremely good.

The second behavior that allows Bob to flourish in the financial wilderness is his insistence on making all his own decisions when it comes to money. It's not that he doesn't ask for advice—he asked for mine, after all—but he doesn't give up control of his investments to anyone. This is not necessarily the practical answer for everyone, particularly those of you who don't have the time, skill, or motivation to get deeply involved in managing your own finances. However, as HFW Principle #3 says, you should make sure everyone helping you with your money is 100 percent on your side. From Bob's perspective, the one person he is *sure* is 100 percent on his side is himself.

I couldn't agree more.

Chapter 14
Tools That You Can Use

As any experienced outdoorsman will tell you, when you backpack in the mountains, other than your hiking shoes and your knowledge of yourself and your own capabilities, the most important equipment to have with you is a good trail map. You also need a flashlight, a compass to know where you are, and perhaps a pair of binoculars to survey the terrain around you (assuming you can get high enough to get a clear view of where you are). I hope that this book has given you those tools.

Now, though, it is time to fill your backpack with other items that may be useful as you make your way into the wilderness. This is not an exhaustive list of what to carry with you, but the assets I have described below are ones I have found useful and would suggest that you consider for yourself.

Real Estate – A Source of Food and Shelter for Survival

The single biggest asset that most people own is their home. This source of wealth is far bigger than what people generally have in their 401(k) or other retirement savings accounts. As of 2016, the Urban Institute reported that the value of total net home equity (house value minus the mortgage) that Americans had access to was about *$11 trillion*.[129] This amount is almost twice as much as the $5.7 trillion[130] of defined contribution—that is, 401(k), 403(b), among others—balances reported on government filings in the same year.

Unlike other financial assets that we have talked about throughout this book, your home is not "spendable" in the same way that a bank account is or even as liquid as your stocks and bonds that can be easily sold and turned into cash very quickly. That being said, your home should be considered an essential part of your financial situation and incorporated directly into your strategy for financial health.

This should not be news to anyone, and in fact, many financial planners opine at length about what you should do with your home. I'm not going to do that, because I don't know you and I don't know your situation.

I will tell you this, though. Ever since I bought my first condo in 1980, I have used the equity in my home(s) for many purposes. Here are some of the ways I have used that extremely important asset:

1. As a place for me and my family to live
2. As shelter for guests or others in my community who needed a place to live temporarily while they rebuilt their financial lives
3. As a source of ready cash by setting up a home equity line of credit (HELOC)
4. As a means of building my capacity to take on other debt (both as collateral and as a means to improve my credit rating)
5. As a means to build wealth through cash out refinancing, which allowed me to invest in other assets (including a second home)
6. As a means of generating income by renting out parts, or all, of my houses (on both a long-term and short-term basis)
7. As a means of generating business income (using a home office and, more recently, by selling the grapes that grew on my farm in Sonoma)

There are other creative ways to use the value of your home to enhance your financial wellness (e.g., as collateral for starting a business or to keep one going), but these are just the ones I have used in my life. Before we move on to other tools, I want to note two more uses of my home equity that I haven't utilized yet but may in the future.

First, as we discussed in Chapter 6, your home can be used as a critical component in your retirement income strategy. Specifically, once you are age sixty-two, you can take out a reverse mortgage or home equity conversion mortgage (HECM) and use it not just to supplement your retirement income in a prudent way, but also as a contingency against needing long-term care.

Finally, as many of us would like to leave a legacy for our children, home equity can provide a tax-effective way of providing your heirs with not just a place to live, but also a head start on *their* quest for financial wellness.

Permanent Life Insurance – A Financial Swiss Army Knife

It was 1979. I had just graduated from college and was working as an actuarial student at Connecticut General Life Insurance (CG) when I met my first life insurance salesman, John Greer. He was not a colleague or a workshop leader assigned to teach me the actuarial intricacies of any particular CG product. Rather, he was a Northwestern Mutual Life sales agent barely out of college himself attempting to sell me, a single twenty-three-year-old guy, permanent life insurance. How he came up with the idea to infiltrate another insurance company (CG had its own line of policies) to sell insurance to actuarial students, I will never know. Clearly, though, John was an "out of the box" thinker who was well worth knowing.

The fact is that John closed that sale, and over the next twenty years, I went on to buy four more policies from him, all of which I still own today. This may say something about John and his ability to sell, but I think, even more importantly, it says something about the power and versatility of what is perhaps one of the actuarial profession's greatest inventions and an important contribution to society—the humble life insurance policy.

The concept of life insurance goes back to Roman times, but the life insurance policy as we know it today was created by UK actuaries at the Equitable Life Assurance Society in 1762.[131] It was a company that flourished for over two hundred years until it was undone in the early 2000s by straying into the dangerous waters of guaranteeing the seemingly safe interest rate of 7 percent on almost $10 billion of annuity liability.

Despite being owned by vast numbers of individuals and organizations, life insurance is almost certainly the least understood of the standard financial instruments that individuals and organizations (private, public, and not-for-profit) use in the financial management of their enterprises. More importantly, it can also be a critical component of any individual's plan to achieve holistic financial wellness. The reason for this is simple. Over time, a life insurance policy can perform many different interrelated functions that will help ensure your financial wellness. These include capital accumulation, tax minimization, family protection, estate planning, and even cash flow management. It may not be the best at any particular function, but with so many different features, life insurance can be used for different purposes at different times in your life. It is always a good tool to have for when a particular need arises. In short, life insurance is the Swiss army knife of financial products, always available and usually sufficient to get the job done.

The history of life insurance and the twists and turns of how its various uses evolved is in and of itself a fascinating story but well beyond the scope of this book. Today, there are many different types of life insurance, with the three most important being guaranteed renewable term (GRT), variable universal life (VUL), and whole life. GRT and VUL are extremely valuable products, and both can be used by organizations as well as individuals for financial management, but the one most relevant for our purposes (i.e., to help you survive in the financial wilderness) is whole life.

In my view, whole life insurance has been subject to a great deal of unfair criticism. And yet, it is one of the most important tools available to ensure your holistic financial wellness.

I bought whole life insurance from John when I was twenty-three. For a young person just starting out in the world, it can be one of the smartest purchases you will ever make. For almost forty years, I paid a small premium every month into a vehicle that provided me with both insurance protection and a tax-sheltered investment. Some of my premium went to paying for a death benefit (the "cost of insurance"), but the vast majority went to the cash value, which was an investment account that received guaranteed interest, and which accumulated, tax-free. Initially, the death benefit was very modest ($20,000 if I remember right) but with the additional policies I purchased in the ensuing years, the death benefit ultimately grew to almost $1 million.

Thankfully, it never got paid. Even though I survived, and in some sense a portion of my premiums were "wasted," the presence of that protection gave my wife and son the significant comfort of knowing that, in the event of my untimely demise, they would be taken care of. That comfort (and the steps that my wife did not have to take as a result) contributed to our family's

financial wellness and should not be underestimated. Furthermore, because I was so young when I bought the policy, the cost of insurance was very modest and continued that way for the life of the policy. In fact, even after considering that cost of insurance, the cash value accumulated at a compound tax free annual rate of almost 6 percent. As of last year, that "forced savings account" was worth more than $400,000.

My policies, however, were even more valuable than that. As my financial life got more complicated and I moved from city to city, bought and sold houses, got married, divorced, and married again, there were times when I needed cash, sometimes a lot more cash than I had readily available. I was able to borrow (essentially from myself) amounts I needed from the policy and pay myself back over a period of time and at a rate that was completely within my control. In short, the cash value provided a buffer that allowed me to get over the "liquidity bumps" that we all face as we make our way through life.

At the end of 2016, I retired from full-time consulting. Just before I did, I converted my policies into "reduced paid-up status." As a result, two more extraordinary features of my policies have come into focus, each of which will be extremely valuable to me in the years ahead. First, about half of my $400,000 cash value is considered "cost basis" that I can withdraw and spend any time I want and never pay tax on it. It is a powerful source of emergency savings that I can tap into should an unforeseen contingency arise.

Second, and even more importantly, I now have a guaranteed death benefit of $800,000 that will go to my wife (or another beneficiary if she dies first), tax-free. If I were to try and buy such a benefit today, it would be extremely expensive; it might not even be available to me without undergoing a full medical exam. This is not only valuable in and of itself, but that $800,000 death benefit has allowed us to withdraw more from our 401(k) savings than otherwise, because we know that we only have to use that money while I am alive. After I am gone, the life insurance will take care of the rest. It is this security against future contingencies as well as the current liquidity it offers that make whole life insurance a valuable part of what has allowed me to achieve and maintain my financial health.

RIGs – What You Need to Start a Fire and Keep You Warm

In Chapter 6, we discussed some of the truth seekers you should look to for information you can trust. We made reference to Steve Vernon,[132] a former colleague of mine who, after he retired, started a consulting firm called Rest of Life Communications, where he focused on what individuals of all walks of life can do after they retire to maintain a reasonable standard of living.

In his many books on planning for retirement, Steve talks about retirement income generators (RIGs) and describes several that everyone should be aware of. Steve's books are well worth reading for anyone who wants to plan for retirement, but for our purposes, the most important of his RIGs are guaranteed and variable annuities. Like the whole life insurance policies described above, annuities were invented by insurance companies. The concept of providing a guaranteed lifetime stream of payments goes back centuries, but the first annuity product that individuals could buy on their own was issued by the Pennsylvania Company for Insurance on Lives and Granting Annuities[133] in 1912; large insurance companies like Hancock, Met, and Prudential still dominate the market today. In some ways, annuities are the mirror image of life insurance. Whole life insurance will, among other things, protect the financial wellness of your family in the event you die before your time; however, annuities will protect you and your family's wellbeing in the event you live *too long*.

We discussed annuities at some length in Chapter 8, where I described how they can be used as one side of a potential barbell strategy that you might use throughout your life to ensure a safe and steady amount of guaranteed income that you can rely on if all else fails. They are insurance of another kind, not quite as versatile as whole life insurance, but certainly a useful tool along with other RIGs that belong in your backpack.

Planned Gifts – Leaving a Cache for Others Who Come After You

If you are like most people, you care a lot about what happens after you leave this world. Except for the very wealthy, very few of us (and even fewer financial planners) really take a hard look at what this implies for how we should manage our financial life both before and after we retire. As a practical matter, when it comes to financial decisions, what this means is that not only should you consider those scenarios where you don't exhaust all your assets, but you should also think about other financial steps that you can take to leave something behind.

In addition to your house and life insurance, there is one other mechanism for leaving a legacy that you should consider. Just like thoughtful hikers who leave a cache of food or blankets for others to use when they move on up the trail, Planned Gifts can allow someone of only modest means to provide for the next generation.

Planned Gifts can be used to *both* generate retirement income *and* leave a legacy. There are two main types that do this—charitable gift annuity (CGA) and charitable remainder trust (CRT). While a CGA is considered a gift by the philanthropic community, it can also be considered as a not-so-traditional retirement planning tool. We talked above about how effective annuities in general can be in ensuring your financial health. In some ways, CGAs operate like any other annuity that you can buy from an insurance company. However, instead of allowing a big corporation to make money on your purchase, the profits on a CGA go to the charity that you got it from. You can obtain a CGA from almost any large not-for-profit organization, university, or charity. I purchased one from my old school, but many people get them from large charities whose mission they believe in.

In order to get a CGA, you must first make sure the charity of your choice has a CGA program. To find out, just call them up and ask for their Planned Giving department. After you transfer funds to the organization you have chosen, they will provide you (based on a legally binding contract) a guaranteed stream of payments starting either now or at some specified date in the future. Those payments will continue for the rest of your life. The only difference between this and an annuity purchased from an insurance company is that, in addition to the guaranteed lifetime income you get, you *also* receive an immediate tax deduction for the present value of what the charity expects to recover from the transfer after you die and all of the annuity payments had been made.

In essence, obtaining a CGA allows you to provide yourself guaranteed retirement income, leave a legacy, *and* get an immediate tax deduction for the profits that otherwise would have gone to an insurance company had you bought a more traditional annuity. To my mind, a CGA is a great way to invest your retirement savings in a vehicle that can play an integral role in your decumulation strategy while at the same time benefiting a cause you believe in.

CRTs operate in a similar way to CGAs, but they are not quite as secure. While a charity issuing a CGA guarantees your payments for life, a CRT will only make those payments so long as the amount you give the charity (along with the interest it earns after you make your gift) is sufficient to pay your benefits. Either vehicle, however, can convert extra assets you may have accumulated into a stream of retirement income, while at the same time providing you with a tax deduction and leaving a legacy to help make the world a better place.

CGAs and CRTs can be expensive and tricky to obtain, though. If you want to know more about planned giving, read Chapter 12 of *What's Your Future Worth?* and get the full story of my CGA purchase. In that chapter, as well as throughout that book and this one, the message is the same—by all means, ask experts you trust for help in imagining the future and evaluating what *might* occur. However, don't *ever* let others set your personal rate of discount by telling you how much (or how little) value to place on what you get/give today vs. what comes your way tomorrow or even in the distant future when you are gone.

Chapter 15
Concluding Thoughts

"Money is like fire. It can cook your food and help you survive the night, but it can also burn your house down and destroy all that you have." —From a conversation with my wife in 1996

Life Assurances and the Real Meaning of Money

It is acutely ironic that just as I was putting the finishing touches on this manuscript, feeling that I had effectively communicated my knowledge about how to live in the Money Mountain wilderness and, in particular, how to avoid and survive financial forest fires, a real forest fire roared through Sonoma County where I live and burned my home to the ground. I had fifteen minutes to evacuate, and in that short time, I had to make some of the hardest decisions of my life.

In that quarter of an hour, I had to make not one, but hundreds of decisions. Specifically, I had to decide what of my possessions to take and what to leave behind. In every room, on every surface, in every drawer and in every bookcase were things of different shapes, sizes, and values. The value of each was a mix of both monetary and emotional. Almost every object in the house reflected a combination of meaning and functionality. It was an impossibly difficult algebra problem—a gigantic set of simultaneous equations that had too many variables and no unique solution.

And it wasn't just that I had only a frighteningly short amount of time to choose. There was also the problem of packing. What would fit in my car, how long would it take to gather and pack, and where would I keep it when I got to where I was going?

Fortunately, I didn't panic, and I knew enough about deadlines to make my choices and fill my Toyota Tacoma with enough time left to get off my property, down the dirt road where I live, and onto the highway before the flames arrived.

I put my passport, my will, some family photos, and my three laptops into a suitcase along with as many of my notebooks and journals as I could carry down from my loft. Then I threw some clothes in a gym bag that was lying on my bedroom floor. Finally, on my way out, I picked up some memorabilia, including an album of 1960s baseball cards, two or three Grateful Dead Concert ticket stubs, and some childhood memories. And then I grabbed two books.

The first was Taleb's math book on fat-tailed distributions that I needed in order to complete this book, and the second was the most important book I owned—a first edition *Assurance of Lives* by Charles

Babbage. It was objectively important, yes, but also the one out of all the hundreds of treasured books I used to have that meant the most to me.

Babbage is best known as one of the inventors of the electronic computer, but he was also one of the founders of actuarial science.[134] While the first life insurance company was formed in 1762[135] and Edmond Halley (of Halley's Comet) produced the first Life Table in 1693,[136] it was Babbage who first laid out the key principles of actuarial science in *Assurance of Lives* in 1826.[137] Several years ago, my sister gave me a rare first edition of this monumental work, and it was that book (photo at the beginning of this chapter) that I saved from the ravages of the Glass Fire that consumed everything else I left behind.

More than its monetary value, which is considerable, Babbage's work represented to me the essence of the actuarial perspective and why I believe it is so important today. As actuaries, we contemplate the intersection of time, risk, and money. We try to balance all three to understand where we are and determine how to move forward into the future in a way that will assure us that our lives are lived in as secure and safe a manner as possible in this uncertain, complex, and dangerous world.

What is Value?

Even though I had sufficient fire insurance to compensate me monetarily for my losses, the impact of the fire was devastating and destroyed much more of my treasure than could be replaced by money. The choices I had to make brought into razor-sharp focus the question of what is value and what we really need to sustain ourselves. I knew that my money was safe in the four banks I keep it in, that most of my critical records were stored electronically on the three laptops I grabbed on my way out the door (I do believe in redundancy), but suddenly, both my past (i.e., memories) and my future (income, living space, and all the things that keep me comfortable) were gone.

It has now been almost two months since the fire, and my perspective on the meaning of the value of goods and services has broadened considerably. I spoke in Chapter 2 about what money is, but our things, skills, and the way we deploy both have value that can't always be translated into dollars. This is not news to anyone, but what happened to my home delivered this lesson to me in the most compelling way imaginable.

What I learned is that value comes from what can be *done* with things and skills. That value is determined in part by what they can do for us and what they can do for others. It is the doing for others that led to the invention of money. The transfer of value back and forth between people has led to the Money Mountain wilderness, which is the subject of this book.

Throughout this book, I have explicitly refrained from venturing any opinion on how the world of money *should* work. To me, the essence of the actuarial perspective is to observe, analyze, and opine on what *is* and not to make recommendations for what would make it better. The mission of the Society of Actuaries has been to "substitute facts for impressions," and I don't intend to start making economic policy recommendations now. But I will say this:

Money is a human invention. It really has no material basis, and yet it is one of mankind's most clever and creative inventions. As the quote at the beginning of the chapter suggests, money is less a thing and more a form of energy, one that has allowed us to build a world in which billions of us can live and sustain ourselves.

Money has a dark side, however. Being a human invention and a form of energy, it also has the potential to cause great damage to ourselves and the environment in which we live. Some of that may be a result of the inherent properties of what money is, but it may also be due to the fact that almost all money moves from one party to another as a result of *tr*ansactions that are based on rights, obligations, and contracts (both explicit and implicit) between people.

That may seem an unavoidable consequence of what money is and how people need to use it, but there is another way. Specifically, people can sustain themselves via *gifts*, which are given freely from one human being to another. In the last two months, I have experienced this first-hand as my family and friends in Sonoma have provided me an extraordinary amount of help (services and things) to help me get back on my feet. The outpouring of support has been overwhelming, and I can only hope that one day I can reciprocate.

In fact, many societies have based their entire economies on the principle of giving and receiving gifts. Such a system is called a *gift economy*, and when it works, it does so because of *reciprocity* and not obligation. Anyone who has spent time at a Grateful Dead concert or attended the Burning Man Festival in Nevada knows that a gift economy can work. Whether it is scalable or can work in society in general is a harder question, and one that I am singularly unqualified to answer. Still, it is something to contemplate.

In the meantime, let us hope that those who have the responsibility to tinker with the system are clever and creative enough to keep the dangers of money from causing too much damage and, if necessary, to implement changes that will ultimately make it more resilient and even antifragile.

In the end, money is one of the most important things we use to facilitate our material lives and to make and keep healthy the relationships we have with those we care about.

If there is one thing you should take away from this book, it is that our financial system is not only orders of magnitude more complex than our individual situations, but it is also orders of magnitude vaster than anyone of us can ever view or comprehend. And so, as you make your way through it, hopefully with a copy of *Money Mountaineering* in your backpack, remember that wherever you want to go, you have to get there one step at a time.

As the Chinese proverb says: "A journey of a thousand miles begins with a single step."

May your next step be the right one.

Endnotes

INTRODUCTION

1.   TIAA-CREFF stands for the Teachers Insurance and Annuity Association of America-College Retirement Equities Fund.

2.   Blog postings going back to November 2014 are available on my website: http://www.peterneuwirth.com.

3.   Inflation, consumer prices (annual percent) - United States, Data from the World Bank, https://data.worldbank.org/indicator/FP.CPI.TOTL. ZG?locations=US.

4.   History of Debt and Interest, *Stack Exchange*, https://economics.stackexchange. com/questions/6970/when-was-fractional-reserve-banking-introduced.

5.   Tim Sandle, "Using big data to predict the future," *Digital Journal*, December 2, 2018, http://www.digitaljournal.com/tech-and-science/technology/ using-big-data-to-predict-the-future/article/538144#:~:text=Advances%20 with%20machine%20learning%20and,new%20application%20looks%20 at%20medici.

6.   Nassim Taleb, *Statistical Consequences of Fat Tails: Real World Preasymptotics, Epistemology, and Applications* (STEM Academic Press, Illustrated edition, 2020), 1–419.

7.   Nassim Taleb, *Antifragile: Things that Gain from Disorder* (New York: Random House, 2012), 92.

8.   Annie Duke, *Thinking in Bets: Making Smarter Decisions When You Don't Have All the Facts* (New York: Penguin Random House, 2018), 1–231.

9.   Marginal utility is defined by the *Economist* as "how much extra utility a person gets from consuming (or doing) an extra unit of something," https:// www.economist.com/economics-a-to-z/m#node-21529419.

10.   Nassim Taleb, *Antifragile: Things that Gain from Disorder* (New York: Random House, 2012), 389.

175

CHAPTER 1

11 James Chen, "Bear Stearns," *Investopedia*, last modified May 15, 2020, https://www.investopedia.com/terms/b/bear-stearns.asp#:~:text=Bear%20 Stearns%20was%20a%20New,leverage%20led%20to%20its%20demise.

12 See: en.wikipedia.org/wiki/American_International_Group.

13 *Ibid.*

14 Roddy Boyd, *Fatal Risk: A Cautionary Tale of AIG's Corporate Suicide* (Hoboken, Wiley 2011).

15 Michael Lewis, *The Big Short: Inside the Doomsday Machine* (New York, W. W. Norton & Company, 2010) n.p.

18 Adam McKay, *The Big Short* (December 11, 2015; Los Angeles: Paramount Pictures, 2015), DVD.

16 Nassim Taleb, *Antifragile: Things that Gain from Disorder* (New York: Random House, 2012), 20.

17 See: en.wikipedia.org/wiki/Rogers_Commission_Report.

18 Watch Richard Feynman's demonstration on YouTube here: https://www.youtube.com/watch?v=raMmRKGkGD4.

19 See: https://en.wikipedia.org/wiki/Space Shuttle Columbia disaster.

20 Nassim Taleb, *Antifragile: Things that Gain from Disorder* (New York: Random House, 2012), 3-5.

21 Nassim Taleb, *The Black Swan: The Impact of the Highly Improbable* (New York: Random House, 2007), xxxii.

CHAPTER 2

22 Adam Hayes, "Dutch Tulip Bulb Market Bubble Definition," *Investopedia*, last modified September, 29, 2020, https://www.investopedia.com/terms/d/dutch tulip bulb market bubble.asp.

23 See: en.wikipedia.org/wiki/South_Sea_Company.

24 The Dow Jones Industrial Index was $824.57 on January 2, 1980 and was $2,002.25 on January 8, 1987.

25 Nick Lioudis, "What is the Gold Standard?" *Investopedia*, last modified September, 24, 2020, https://www.investopedia.com/ask/answers/09/gold-standard.asp.

26 History.com, "Gold Prices Soar," last modified January 13, 2020, https://www.history.com/this-day-in-history/gold-prices-soar.

27 Adam Hayes, "Black Monday Definition," *Investopedia*, last modified November 30, 2020, https://www.investopedia.com/terms/b/blackmonday.asp.

28   Murray N. Rothbard, "Aristotle on Private Property and Money," Mises Institute, accessed January 11, 2021, https://mises.org/library/aristotl e-private-property-and-money#:~:text=Aristotle%2C%20however%2C%20 created%20great%20trouble,and%20cannot%20itself%20increase%20 wealth.

29   See: https://www.britannica.com/topic/Amsterdamsche-Wisselbank.

30   Frank Capra, *It's a Wonderful Life* (January 7, 1947, Los Angeles: Liberty Films, 1946), Film.

31   Jeff Desjardins, "This Stunning Visualization Shows All of the World's Money," Business Insider, last Modified December 20, 2015, https://www. businessinsider.com/all-of-worlds-money-in-one-chart-2015-12#:~:text= This%20includes%20the%20global%20supply,the%20equivalent%20 of%20US%20dollars.

32   See: https://en.wikipedia.org/wiki/Gold_reserve.

33   Douglas Hofstadter, *Gödel, Escher, Bach: An Eternal Golden Braid* (New York: Basic Books, 1979), 1–777.

CHAPTER 3

34   A PDF of the original 1982 publication by SRI International, written by Leslie Lamport, Robert Shostak, and Marshall Pease, is available at https://www.mi crosoft.com/en-us/research/uploads/prod/2016/12/The-Byzantine-Generals-Problem.pdf.

35   Jamie Redman, "Triple-Entry Bookkeeping: How Satoshi Nakamoto Solved the Byzantine Generals' Problem," *Bitcoin News*, August 2, 2020, https://news. bitcoin.com/triple-entry-bookkeeping-how-satoshi-nakamoto-solved-the-b yzantine-generals-problem/.

36   Beginning in the Fall of 2020, Bitcoin began to rise from $10,000 to a value of $40,000 by January 8th 2021.

37   Bernard Lietaer, *The Future of Money* (New York: Random House, 2001).

38   Bernard Lietaer, *The Future of Money*, 73.

39   Bernard Lietaer, *The Future of Money*, 73–111.

40   *Ibid.*

41   Bernard Lietaer, *The Future of Money*, 91.

42   Nassim Taleb, *Antifragile: Things that Gain from Disorder* (New York: Random House, 2012), 85–88.

43   See: en.wikipedia.org/wiki/Indigenous_peoples_of_California.

44   Ruchir Agarwal and Signe Krogstrup, "Cashing In: How to Make Negative Interest Rates Work," *IMFBlog*, last modified February 5, 2019, https://blogs. imf.org/2019/02/05/cashing-in-how-to-make-negative-interest-rates-work/.

45   See: en.wikipedia.org/wiki/Modern_Monetary_Theory.

46   Stephanie Kelton, *The Deficit Myth: Modern Monetary Theory and the Birth of the People's Economy* (New York: Public Affairs, 2020).

CHAPTER 4

47   Sylvia Porter, *Money Book: How to Earn It, Spend It, Save It, Invest It, Borrow It, and Use It to Better Your Life* (New York: Avon Books, 1976), 8.

48   Helaine Olen, *Pound Foolish: Exposing the Dark Side of the Personal Finance Industry* (New York: Penguin House, 2012).

49   Jason Zweig, "Suze Orman Parts Ways With Newsletter," *The Wall Street Journal*, April 24, 2012, https://www.wsj.com/articles/BL-TOTALB-516.

50   Helaine Olen, *Pound Foolish: Exposing the Dark Side of the Personal Finance Industry* (New York: Penguin House, 2012), 27–48.

51   Sue Asci, "Saving with Suze and TD Ameritrade," *InvestmentNews*, September 27, 2009, https://www.investmentnews.com/saving-with-suze-and-td-ameritrade-24189.

52   Jason Zweig, "Meet Suze Orman's Newsletter Guru," *The Wall Street Journal*, January 21, 2012, https://www.wsj.com/articles/SB10001424052970203750404577173344073389960.

53   Ron Lieber, "Suze Orman's Approved Prepaid Debit Cards Are Quietly Discontinued," *The New York Times*, last Modified June 16, 2014, https://www.nytimes.com/2014/06/17/business/suze-ormans-approved-prepaid-debit-cards-are-quietly-discontinued.html.

54   Bobby Ross Jr., "Ocala Star-Banner - Google News Archive Search,". *news.google.com*, retrieved January 14, 2021, https://news.google.com/newspapers?nid=1356&dat=20030331&id=VLtNAAAAIBAJ&pg=6793,8240090.

55   Dave Ramsey, "Is Money Evil?", excerpt from Dave Ramsey's Radio Show, Audio 36:52, https://www.daveramsey.com/askdave/leaving-a-legacy/is-money-evil.

56   Dave Ramsey, *The Total Money Makeover: A Proven Plan for Financial Fitness* (Nashville: Nelson Books, 2003), 104–124.

57   *Ibid.*

58   *Ibid.*

59   Dave Ramsey, *The Total Money Makeover: A Proven Plan for Financial Fitness*, 120.

60   Dave Ramsey, *The Total Money Makeover: A Proven Plan for Financial Fitness*, xv.

61   Sylvia Porter, *Money Book: How to Earn It, Spend It, Save It, Invest It, Borrow It, and Use It to Better Your Life* (New York: Avon Books, 1976), 8.

62   "Company History," Media Relations, Daveramsey.com, https://www.daveramsey.com/pr/company-history.

63   "Endorsed Local Providers Program," Daveramsey.com, https://www.daveramsey.com/elp.

CHAPTER 5

64   Ric Edelman, *The Truth About Your Future: The Money Guide You Need Now, Later, and Much Later* (New York: Simon & Schuster, 2017).

65   Wes Moss, *You Can Retire Sooner Than You Think* (New York: McGraw-Hill Education, 2014), 3–15.

66   *Ibid.*

67   *Ibid.*

68   Wes Moss, *You Can Retire Sooner Than You Think*, 16.

69   Wes Moss, *You Can Retire Sooner Than You Think*, 5.

70   Wes Moss, *You Can Retire Sooner Than You Think*, x.

71   Wes Moss, *You Can Retire Sooner Than You Think*, 97–114.

72   Einstein is widely reputed to have said this, but there is no official record of him making such a statement.

73   Dave Ramsey, *The Total Money Makeover: A Proven Plan for Financial Fitness* (Nashville: Nelson Books, 2003), 104–124.

74   David Bach, *The Latte Factor: Why You Don't Have to Be Rich to Live Rich* (New York: Simon & Schuster, 2019).

CHAPTER 6

75   HSBC stands for Hongkong and Shanghai Banking Corporation.

76   The Employee Retirement Income Security Act (ERISA) of 1974 is a federal law that sets minimum standards for most voluntarily established retirement and health plans in private industry to provide protection for individuals in these plans, U.S. Dept. of Labor, https://www.dol.gov/general/topic/health-plans/erisa.

77   Barry H. Sacks and Stephen R. Sacks, 2012, "Reversing the Conventional Wisdom: Using Home Equity to Supplement Retirement Income," *Journal of Financial Planning* 25(2): 43.

78   Marguerita M. Cheng, Blue Ocean Global Wealth, https://www.blueocean-globalwealth.com/our-team.php.

79   Shelley Giordano, Academy for Home Equity in Financial Planning, University of Illinois at Urbana-Champaign, https://ahe.illinois.edu/about/members/giordano/.

80   Wade D. Pfau, American College of Financial Services, https://www.theamericancollege.edu/our-people/faculty/wade-pfau.

CHAPTER 7

81   John Keats, "Letter to George and Thomas Keats," December 21, 1817.

82   "July 1654: Pascal's Letters to Fermat on the 'Problem of Points,'" American Physics Society News, July 2009 (Vol. 18, Num. 7), https://www.aps.org/publications/apsnews/200907/physicshistory.cfm.

83   Desmond Clarke, "Blaise Pascal", *The Stanford Encyclopedia of Philosophy* (Fall 2015 Edition), Edward N. Zalta (ed.), accessed Jan.15 2021, https://plato.stanford.edu/archives/fall2015/entries/pascal.

84   Nassim Nicholas Taleb and Avital Pilpel, "On the Unfortunate Problem of the Nonobservability of the Probability Distribution," First Draft, 2001, This version, 2004, https://www.fooledbyrandomness.com/knowledge.pdf.

85   See: en.wikipedia.org/wiki/Pareto_principle.

CHAPTER 8

86   Nassim Taleb, *Antifragile: Things that Gain from Disorder* (New York: Random House, 2012), 159-160.

87   See: en.wikipedia.org/wiki/Nassim_Nicholas_Taleb#Praise_and_criticism.

88   Peter Neuwirth, *What's Your Future Worth?* (Oakland: Berrett-Koehler Publishers, 2015).

89   See: en.wikipedia.org/wiki/Extreme_value_theory.

90   Nassim Taleb, *The Bed of Procrustes: Philosophical and Practical Aphorisms* (New York: Random House, 2010), 76.

CHAPTER 9

91   Dave Bingham has written several books on rock-climbing in Idaho including, for example, *Idaho Underground* (New Castle: Wolverine 2016).

92   Ginia Bellafante, "Dealt a Bad Hand? Fold 'em. Then Raise." *New York Times*, January 19, 2006, https://www.nytimes.com/2006/01/19/garden/dealt-a-bad-hand-fold-em-then-raise.html.

93   The NBC National Heads-Up tournament was held from 2005–2011 and in 2013. Annie Duke won in 2010.

94   Annie Duke, *Thinking in Bets: Making Smarter Decisions When You Don't Have All the Facts* (New York: Penguin Random House, 2018), 1–231.

95   Annie Duke, *Thinking in Bets: Making Smarter Decisions When You Don't Have All the Facts*, 28.

96   Jim O'Shaughnessy and Jamie Catherwood, "Annie Duke – How to Decide (EP.22)" *Infiniteloops Podcast*, Oct. 15, 2020, 1:21:01, https://www.infiniteloopspodcast.com/annie-duke-how-to-decide-ep22/.

97   Annie Duke, *Thinking in Bets: Making Smarter Decisions When You Don't Have All the Facts* (New York: Penguin Random House, 2018), 37.

98   Annie Duke, *Thinking in Bets: Making Smarter Decisions When You Don't Have All the Facts*.

99   Annie Duke, *Thinking in Bets: Making Smarter Decisions When You Don't Have All the Facts*, 8.

100   Adam Hayes, "Time-Preference Theory of Interest," *Investopedia*, last updated January 31, 2020, https://www.investopedia.com/terms/t/time-preference-theory-of-interest.asp.

101   Emily Brandon, "An Innovative Way to Face Retirement," *U.S. News: Money*, January 14, 2013, https://money.usnews.com/money/retirement/articles/2013/01/14/an-innovative-way-to-face-retirement.

CHAPTER 10

102   "10 Year Treasury Rate - 54 Year Historical Chart," *Macrotrends.net*, accessed January 21, 2021, https://www.macrotrends.net/2016/10-year-treasury-bond-rate-yield-chart.

103   James Chen, "Modern Portfolio Theory (MPT)," *Investopedia*, last modified March 1, 2021, https://www.investopedia.com/terms/m/modernportfolio-theory.asp.

104   Amos Tversky and Daniel Kahneman, "Rational Choice and the Framing of Decisions," *The Journal of Business*, 59(4) (1986): 251–278.

105 Peter Neuwirth, "The Time Value of Time," *Contingencies,* January 1997, http://www.peterneuwirth.com/wp-content/uploads/2014/12/TimeValueof Time.pdf.

106 See: en.wikipedia.org/wiki/Richard_Thaler

107 Michael Lewis, *The Undoing Project: A Friendship That Changed Our Minds* (New York: W.W. Norton & Co., 2016).

108 Michael Lewis, *The Big Short: Inside the Doomsday Machine* (New York, W. W. Norton & Company, 2010), n.p.

109 Adam McKay, *The Big Short* (December 11, 2015; Los Angeles: Paramount Pictures, 2015), DVD.

110 Michael Lewis, *Liar's Poker* (New York: W.W. Norton & Company, 1989).

111 Michael Lewis, *Flash Boys: A Wall Street Revolt* (New York: W.W. Norton & Company, 2014).

112 Peter Neuwirth, "The Time Value of Time," *Contingencies,* January 1997, http://www.peterneuwirth.com/wp-content/uploads/2014/12/TimeValueof Time.pdf.

113 Andrew B. Abel, University of Pennsylvania Finance Department, https://fnce.wharton.upenn.edu/profile/abel/.

114 Richard Thaler, "Some Empirical Evidence on Dynamic Inconsistency," *Economics Letters,* Vol. 8.3, (1981), 201–207, https://doi.org/10.1016/0165-1765(81)90067-7.

115 Susan Kelley, "A 'Playful' Nobel Prize Winner Laid Groundwork for His Field at Cornell," *Cornell Chronicle,* October 11, 2017, https://news.cornell.edu/stories/2017/10/playful-nobel-prize-winner-laid-groundwork-his-field-cornell.

116 Daniel Kahneman, Jack L. Knetsch, and Richard H. Thaler, "Anomalies: The Endowment Effect, Loss Aversion, and Status Quo Bias," *Journal of Economic Perspectives,* 5(1) 1991: 193–206.

117 See: en.wikipedia.org/wiki/Stanford marshmallow experiment.

118 Richard Thaler, *Nudge: Improving Decisions About Health, Wealth, and Happiness* (New York: Penguin Books, 2009).

119 Peter Neuwirth, "In Defense of Personal Rates of Discount," July 12, 2015, http://www.peterneuwirth.com/?cat=4

CHAPTER 11

120 See: en.wikipedia.org/wiki/List of cognitive biases and: en.wikipedia.org/wiki/Emotional bias.

121 Annie Duke, *How to Decide: Simple Tools for Making Better Choices* (New York: Portfolio, 2020).

[122] Amos Tversky and Daniel Kahneman, "Judgment under Uncertainty: Heuristics and Biases," *Science*, 185 (4157) (1974): 1124–1131, https://www2.psych.ubc.ca/~schaller/Psyc590Readings/TverskyKahneman1974.pdf.

[123] Justin Kruger and David Dunning, "Unskilled and Unaware of It: How Difficulties in Recognizing One's Own Incompetence Lead to Inflated Self-Assessments," *Journal of Personality and Social Psychology*, 77(6) (1999), 1121–1134, https://doi.org/10.1037/0022-3514.77.6.1121.

[124] Eldar Shafir, Peter Diamond, and Amos Tversky, "Money Illusion," *The Quarterly Journal of Economics*, Volume 112, Issue 2, May 1997, 341–374, https://doi.org/10.1162/003355397555208.

[125] See: en.wikipedia.org/wiki/Conjunction fallacy.

CHAPTER 12

[126] Annie Duke, *Thinking in Bets: Making Smarter Decisions When You Don't Have All the Facts* (New York: Penguin Random House, 2018), 119–149.

[127] Annie Duke, *Thinking in Bets: Making Smarter Decisions When You Don't Have All the Facts*, 137.

[128] Annie Duke, *Thinking in Bets: Making Smarter Decisions When You Don't Have All the Facts*, 138.

CHAPTER 14

[129] Wei Li and Laurie Goodman, "How Much House Do Americans Really Own? Measuring America's Accessible Housing Wealth by Geography and Age," *Urban Institute Research Report*, July 2016, https://www.urban.org/sites/default/files/publication/82556/2016.07.13%20Measuring%20American's%20Net%20Housing%20Wealth final4.pdf.

[130] Lee Barney, "Retirement Fund Assets Grew 8% from 2014 to $19.1 Trillion in 2016," *Plansponsor.com*, March 10, 2017, https://www.plansponsor.com/retirement-fund-assets-grew-8-from-2014-to-19-1-trillion-in-2016/.

[131] "Equitable Life Assurance Society Archive 1762 – 1975," Institute and Faculty of Actuaries, 2007,https://www.actuaries.org.uk/system/files/documents/pdf/ELAS catalogue final Oct 2007B.pdf.

[132] Steve Vernon, The Retirement Income Summit, accessed January 21, 2021, https://theretirementincomesummit.com/speakers/speakers/steve-vernon/.

[133] "History of Annuities," *SaveWealth Financial*, accessed January 21, 2021, https://www.savewealth.com/retirement/annuities/history/.

CHAPTER 15

[134] Anthony Hyman, *Charles Babbage: Pioneer of the Computer,*" Princeton University Press, 1985, https://books.google.com/books?id=YCddaWqWK2cC &pg=PA59/.

[135] Archived from the Original: The Actuarial Profession, "History: Importance of the archive," *Advance Insurance and Benefits,* 2013, https://web.archive. org/web/20140201230156/http://www.advancenv.com/importance-archive/.

[136] Nicolas Bacaër, "Halley's Life Table (1693)," *A Short History of Mathematical Population Dynamics,* 2011, https://doi.org/10.1007/978-0-85729-115-8 2.

[137] Charles Babbage, *A Comparative View of the Various Institutions for the Assurance of Lives* (London: J. Mawman, 1826).

Acknowledgments

One of the sad facts of the publishing world is the necessity of putting together this section of the book before it is actually in print, and so the list of those who helped make *Money Mountaineering* a reality is, of necessity, incomplete. In fact, my book contract originally called for me to submit the Acknowledgments along with my original manuscript. Fortunately, Post Hill Press, and in particular my editor Debby Englander, was understanding enough to extend my deadline until the last possible moment before they asked me to provide an accounting of all the people who helped me with this venture.

And so, my first thank you goes to Debby and her team at PHP who have done all the heavy lifting to turn my musings into a real book. Right behind Debby is my agent Carol Mann who introduced me to PHP and helped me craft my book proposal to overcome the understandable reluctance of the industry to publish a book whose ideas about financial planning are so unorthodox and contrary to conventional wisdom.

Before I go back to the beginning, I want to thank the folks who have helped me to bring this project to completion—Kelsey Page, who provided a complete and thorough first edit, Julia Page, who organized my online presence, which, for an old school actuary like me is a brave new world, and Gabe Guptill, who reconstructed all of my notes on sources and references that were lost in the fire that destroyed my home a few months before my manuscript was due. Gabe's facility with online research, his familiarity with the Chicago Manual of Style footnoting, and his ability to quickly compile and organize my source notes was an invaluable resource.

This book really began with conversations with my writing coach Nico Peck, an extraordinarily gifted teacher and now friend who help me hear my own voice and gave me the confidence to believe that others might want to hear my sometimes contrarian views on financial planning.

From then on, many friends helped by challenging my ideas and reading countless early drafts of different chapters that eventually found their way into the final manuscript. Neil Goldberg, with whom I met regularly to discuss my writing, was the first, but others included Gail Kurtz, Estelle Frankel, David Wallin, and Henry Hecht who had also given me important feedback on my first book and allowed me to "go to the well" again as he provided additional important early feedback on this book.

And then there were my fellow authors, whom I had come to know through my first publisher Berrett-Koehler. Even though I had chosen to have this book published by a different company, the folks at BK, including the company's founder Steve Piersanti, were not only supportive of my efforts, but many of the BK authors generously provided both moral and substantive support to me, making this book far better than it would otherwise have been. In particular, I want to thank Jesse Stoner who, many months ago, when I despaired of ever getting a draft completed, told me that "the book is already written, you just need to transfer it from your brain to paper." Others who provided equally sage advice included Alan Briskin, Stewart Levine, Bob Miglani, Karen Phelan, Marilee Adams, Jennifer Kahnweiler, and many others who I am sure I have forgotten to mention.

Throughout the writing of the book, I was lucky enough to get the insights and ideas of an enormous number of brilliant thinkers and experts in the fields of mathematics, finance, actuarial science, economics, and computer science. These include Steve Vernon, Stefi Baum, Nick Patterson, Eric Baum, James Kenney, Peter Yianilos, Len Charlap, Barry Sacks, Dave Ballard, Tom Herzog, Leland Faust, and most importantly, my father Lee Neuwirth, who, while understandably biased, is not only a great mathematician in his own right, but was also able to help me reach other equally accomplished mathematicians to keep me from making any obvious technical mistakes in areas where I was "driving without a license."

Perhaps the most important of those who helped me hone my ideas and communicate them is Annie Duke. When I first perused Annie's book on one of my visits to Barnes and Noble, I recognized someone who thinks about the same questions I do. I decided right then and there that I had to reach out to her and see if I could find out more about how she thinks about the randomness and incomplete information that we all must deal with. I was surprised and delighted when she responded.

Getting to know Annie and the way she thinks about making decisions under uncertainty has been a tremendous learning opportunity for me. I am deeply grateful both for her powerful insights and her willingness to write the foreword to this book.

I also want to thank all those who shared their experiences and allowed me to tell their stories in the book. I won't name them here because you can read about who they are in the book itself.

For those readers who got all the way through, you know that right in the middle of writing, my home was destroyed by one of the many wildfires that are endemic to Northern California where I live. Without the incredible support and kindness of the community of Santa Rosa, this book would never have seen the light of day. The generosity and compassion provided by the individuals and the community as a whole, as well as the practical help of the many organizations and merchants in town, was beyond valuable in helping me put my life back together and complete my manuscript. They are too numerous to name, and even if I wanted to, some of them never gave me their names.

But here are a few. There was Jesse, Anna, Leon, and Marta who all opened their homes to me when I was a homeless refugee still in shock from the catastrophe that had visited me. There was Linda, Leo, CharylAnn, Terri and Joe—all long-time Santa Rosa natives who had seen many fires and knew just what kind of help, both practical and spiritual, I needed for recovering from what I'd lost. And then there were the shopkeepers and the local folks who always had the time to hear my story and share their own—Randy, Chelsea, and Louisa at Positively 4th Street where I replaced my T-shirts and the other accoutrements of my lifestyle, Sonja at The Furniture Depot who helped me with my furniture needs, Jo at Marta's Vintage Clothing Store in Railroad Square whose work shirts I now wear instead of the ones that burned, Lanny at the Whistle Stop who helped me replace some of my ancient books, and many others whose names I never got.

Before I turn to my family, there is one other person who I need to thank, and that is Patrick Wolfsohn, a contractor who rolled into town last June to visit my resident caretaker, show his daughter what California is like, and pick up a little work while he was here. I hired Patrick to renovate one of the outbuildings on my property and, for reasons I still don't understand, he stayed to fight the fire side by side with Cal Fire until all hope was lost. Beyond all reason, Patrick decided not only to stay and help me rebuild my home, but has also become a business partner, a confidante, and a close friend who has believed in this book from the moment I described it to him back in July, when he wondered what I was doing all day on my computer while he was out sinking posts and sawing lumber.

Finally, there is my family, without whom there would be no book at all. My wife Tali and I are no longer together, but I am still grateful to her, first for our twenty-one years together during which she fully supported my writing and second, for telling me almost immediately after my first book was published that I had another, better book inside me waiting to come out.

Lastly, I want to thank my parents Lee and Sydney, along with my sister Bebe, her husband Chris, and my son Adam. All of them have been a source of steadfast and rock-solid support and encouragement for all that I do. During this incredibly difficult year of the pandemic and other disasters, they have given me a foundation of love and confidence that has allowed me to share my ideas with those who could benefit from hearing about what I have learned in my time in the world of money.

About the Author

Author photo by Patrick Wolfsohn

Peter Neuwirth is an actuary with forty years of experience holding leadership positions at a variety of firms around the country, including most of the major consulting firms (Towers Watson, among others). He now focuses on writing and researching financial wellness issues. He is also the author of the award-winning book, *What's your Future Worth?*